HARMONIZING POWER SYSTEMS IN THE GREATER MEKONG SUBREGION

REGULATORY AND PRICING MEASURES TO FACILITATE TRADE

FEBRUARY 2020

ASIAN DEVELOPMENT BANK

6 ADB Avenue, Mandaluyong City, 1550 Metro Manila, Philippines
Tel +63 2 8632 4444; Fax +63 2 8636 2444
www.adb.org

ISBN 978-92-9262-036-3 (print); 978-92-9262-037-0 (electronic); 978-92-9262-038-7 (ebook)
Publication Stock No. TCS200070
DOI: http://dx.doi.org/10.22617/TCS200070

Notes:
In this publication, "$" refers to United States dollars.
ADB recognizes "China" as the People's Republic of China and "Laos" as the Lao People's Democratic Republic.

Cover design by Rommel Marilla.

Contents

Tables, Figures, and Boxes

Tables

Figures

Boxes

Foreword

In recent years the Greater Mekong Subregion (GMS) has experienced impressive economic growth. This growth has been accompanied by increasing electrification and a growing demand for electricity among domestic, commercial, and industrial customers alike.

Given these developments there has also been growing interest in the GMS to further interconnect member countries' power systems to better facilitate cross-border electricity trading. To this end, for the past decade the Asian Development Bank (ADB) has supported GMS member countries in developing international power trading. In 2010, the foundational study *Facilitating Regional Power Trading and Environmentally Sustainable Development of Electricity Infrastructure in the Greater Mekong Subregion* was completed. Since then, GMS member countries have been working through a Regional Power Trade Coordination Committee supported by ADB to develop international power trading principles and address technical and commercial issues that can ultimately increase trading.

Harmonizing Power Systems in the Greater Mekong Subregion: Regulatory and Pricing Measures to Facilitate Power Trade is a study carried out in close consultation with GMS member countries. It identifies key regulatory and commercial bottlenecks that constrain regional power trade in the subregion, and sets forth a series of practical regulatory and pricing measures that can help overcome these bottlenecks. We hope that some of the proposed measures will help GMS member countries foster greater participation of power sector stakeholders in cross-border power trade.

The findings of this study should be particularly relevant to government ministries and planning departments, regulatory bodies, power utilities, and potential private sector investors that play a critical role in expanding power trading within the subregion.

Ramesh Subramaniam
Director General
Southeast Asia Department

Abbreviations

ACE	area control error
aFRR	automatically activated frequency restoration reserve
AGC	automatic generation control
ASEAN	Association of Southeast Asian Nations
ATC	available transfer capability
BPC	Botswana Power Corporation
CAISO	California Independent System Operator
CSG	China Southern Power Grid Co. Ltd
DAM	day-ahead market
DRC	Democratic Republic of Congo
ECOWAS	Economic Community of West African States
EDL	Electricité du Laos
EDM	Electricidade de Moçambique
EGAT	Electricity Generating Authority of Thailand
EPWA	Energy Purchase and Wheeling Agreement
ERAV	Electricity Regulatory Authority of Viet Nam
ERERA	ECOWAS Regional Electricity Regulation Authority
EVN	Viet Nam Electricity
FCR	frequency containment reserve
FRR	frequency restoration reserve
GCCIA	Gulf Cooperation Centre Interchange Authority
GMS	Greater Mekong Subregion
IGCC	International Grid Control Cooperation
INC	Imbalance Netting Cooperation
IPP	independent power producer

ISO	independent system operator
km	kilometer
Lao PDR	Lao People's Democratic Republic
mFRR	manually activated frequency restoration reserve
MoU	memorandum of understanding
MW	megawatt
MWh	megawatt hour
NERC	North American Electric Reliability Corporation
O&M	operation and maintenance
PJM	Pennsylvania-New Jersey-Maryland
PPA	power purchase agreement
RMR	regional market rules
RPCC	Regional Power Coordination Centre
RPTCC	Regional Power Trade Coordination Committee
RTTM	Regional Transmission Tariff Methodology (RTTM)
SADC	Southern African Development Community
SAPP	Southern African Power Pool
SMO	system and market operator
SNEL	Société Nationale D'électricité
SP	Singapore Power
TNB	Tenaga Nasional Berhad
TSO	transmission system operator
TTC	total transfer capability
WACC	weighted average cost of capital
WAPP	West African Power Pool
WGPG	Working Group on Performance Standards and Grid Codes
WGRI	Working Group on Regulatory Issues
ZESA	Zimbabwe Electricity Supply Authority
ZESCO	Zambia Electricity Supply Corporation

Executive Summary

Countries in the Greater Mekong Subregion (GMS) have identified regional power trading as a priority development area based on ADB's *Study on Regional Power Trade Operating Agreement in the Greater Mekong Subregion*. The study defines four steps—also stated in the Bank's *Greater Mekong Subregion: Energy Sector Assessment, Strategy and Road Map*—toward the development of regional power trading:

- trading through bilateral cross-border connections associated with specific power purchase agreements (PPAs);
- grid-to-grid power trading between any pair of GMS countries, eventually using the transmission facilities of a third country;
- developing transmission links dedicated to cross-border trading; and
- a situation in which most GMS countries have completed the transition to regulatory frameworks with multiple sellers and multiple buyers, to enable a regional wholly competitive market to be implemented.

A commitment to develop the first two stages of regional trading was cemented by the signing of the Inter-governmental Agreement on Regional Power Trade in 2002 and the associated first Memorandum of Understanding in 2005.

Since then, the development of regional power trading has focused on building dedicated transmission lines interconnecting independent power producers (IPPs) in one country with the transmission network of another. The ADB project Facilitating Regional Power Trading and Environmentally Sustainable Development of Electricity Infrastructure in the Greater Mekong Subregion presented a series of technical, system operations, and market design recommendations that provided a framework for the future development of regional power trade through greater interconnection of national power systems. However, regional power trading currently represents less than 2% of the electricity consumption in the GMS.

What then are the barriers preventing a greater uptake of regional power trading, and how can these be overcome? The research that has been undertaken to answer this question highlights a number of areas in which developments are needed to increase regional power trade:

- **promoting an integrated approach to regional power sector planning**, in order to prepare long-term national power development plans collaboratively and promote the increased development of regional power transfers—these benefits need to be fully understood at a regional level if the drive for interconnection and power trading is to increase;

- developing **alternatives to long-term PPAs** to enable more opportunistic trading in the region;
- **improving access to power networks** for IPPs to trade internationally, and for country-to-country trading through the transmission networks of third parties;
- **developing fair and transparent wheeling charges** that will help ensure that the costs incurred by utilities making their network assets available to other parties for international power trading are compensated fairly;
- considering a range of **regulatory arrangements and industry structures**, to recognize international experience and ensure that there are no significant institutional hurdles to increased trading;
- ensuring that **inadvertent energy flows** arising from **imbalances between supply and demand** caused by the non-delivery of regional trades are efficiently identified and accounted for; and
- promoting **increased capacity building** among GMS power utilities to ensure that staff have access to a wide range of international power sector businesses and market operators, and learn how international power trading works.

To further increase power trading in the GMS, a series of measures have been proposed in some key areas.

Open Access

The starting point for developing open access in the GMS is to consider cross-border transmission assets owned by specific IPPs, which are then made available to other generators. Other IPPs must be able to access the transmission lines associated with these projects, to make use of any spare capacity on the existing interconnections for trading purposes. In addition, IPPs must be able to access the national transmission networks in the GMS and to use these to export power to neighbouring countries.

The key requirements for ensuring open access in GMS countries include

- **clear licensing arrangements** for the transmission owner and the system operator in each country, either as independent organizations or as functions within a vertically integrated utility;
- **a license obligation on transmission utilities to offer terms** to new potential generators seeking to generate electricity for domestic consumption, or to export electricity under wheeling arrangements;
- a **transmission connection agreement** that clearly defines the rights and obligations of generators, the transmission owner, and the system operator when a new connection is sought; and
- a **transmission use of system agreement** that supports the right of the generator to be and to remain connected to and energized on the national transmission network.

Both the connection agreement and the use of system agreement should cross-reference a **national grid code, a regional grid code,** and other **technical standards** that govern the connection of generators to the transmission system and the operation of the system with the IPPs. It is essential that both connection and operational issues are covered if the integrity of the transmission system is to be maintained and power system security is not to be compromised.

Methodology for Wheeling Charges

A methodology for wheeling charges is proposed to take into account the use of each transmission asset in GMS regional transmission networks by any wheeling transaction. This approach can be used to allocate the costs of transmission to the relevant trading parties and recover the costs incurred by national utilities in providing wheeling services through their networks. This is important if utilities are to be encouraged to invest in additional transmission to facilitate increased international trade.

The methodology is based on calculated power flows to get an accurate picture of how much transmission capacity each regional trade requires.

This study has developed a detailed methodology that meets the core requirements of recovering the fixed and variable costs of providing wheeling services, including

- a contribution to the **capital costs** of the assets and the recovery of the costs of **depreciation**;
- the recovery of costs associated with **operation and maintenance** of the transmission networks; and
- the costs of **losses** occurring on the transmission systems as a result of wheeling transactions.

Short-Term Bilateral Trading Rules

To develop international power trading beyond trades linked to IPPs holding long-term PPAs with power utilities, short-term bilateral trading rules are needed to complement the longer-term agreements.

To enable trading to take place over a period from a few hours to months ahead, several components of an overall methodology are required. These comprise

- a method for assessing the **available transfer capability** (ATC) on interconnectors, after taking account of long-term bilateral trades, to ensure that short-term trading is physically possible;
- a **simplified trading mechanism** for proposing short-term bilateral contracts and entering into the associated commercial transactions; and
- simplified **metering and settlement processes** for settling contracted quantities.

As part of this study, procedures have been developed to enable generators and utilities in the GMS to trade electricity more flexibly than is currently the case. These procedures could in the future be automated via an online trading platform, which would connect willing buyers and willing sellers in touch with each other and enable trades to enter at shorter notice and more efficiently than is the case if short-term contracts are repeatedly being negotiated.

Balancing Mechanism

Imbalances that arise between scheduled interchanges on interconnectors and what happens in practice need to be settled to avoid financial deficit on the part of utilities whose networks provide balancing energy services.

Two options exist for settling imbalances:

- **"in-kind"** repayment of energy at times of days and seasons of the year that correspond to those when the imbalance occurred. This will help ensure that the energy replaced has approximately the same value as the energy supplied by the utility providing the balancing service;
- **a cash-based** settlement mechanism, based on an understanding of which power plant(s) provided the balancing service and, therefore, the cost of the energy supplied.

"In-kind" settlement of imbalances has been proposed for application in the GMS initially, but with the development of a cash-based system of cost recovery based on the identification of a generation technology that can provide system support under different loading conditions.

A market for balancing services could be envisaged in the region, giving the opportunity for specific generators to participate in offering prices and quantities of energy to compensate for shortfalls—actual versus scheduled trade volumes.

Coordination of Regional Power Trading

GMS countries signed a memorandum of understanding (MoU) in December 2012 in which they agreed to the formation of the Regional Power Coordination Centre (RPCC). This would have a range of functions focused on promoting the coordinated planning and operation of the national power systems and representing the common interests of GMS countries on matters relating to power trade.

A key finding from this study reinforces the need for the RPCC or a regional market operator that can take responsibility for

- calculating wheeling charges and transmission losses associated with regional power trading;
- publishing potential short-term bilateral trades and undertaking the technical and commercial processes required to assess the ATC on the transmission systems to support short-term bilateral trades;
- carrying out calculations in support of the settlement of inadvertent energy transfers, involving the collection and processing of meter data; and
- potentially acting as an agent to facilitate financial settlement of power trades.

These functions represent a significant extension of the current role played by the GMS Regional Power Trade Coordination Committee (RPTCC). GMS countries therefore need to agree on the practical aspects of establishing the RPCC as an operational organization to fulfill these functions.

All the above proposals and the associated background work are documented in full in the series of reports that have been produced under the ADB project Harmonizing the Greater Mekong Subregion Power Systems to Facilitate Regional Power Trade. The principles presented in this study aim to inform future work in engaging with electricity industry stakeholders regionally and expanding regional power trade.

1 Regional Power Trading in the GMS: Current Situation

Earlier ADB studies defined a roadmap for developing regional power trading in the Greater Mekong Subregion (GMS), including

- trading through bilateral cross-border connections associated with specific power purchase agreements (PPAs);
- grid-to-grid power trading between any pair of GMS countries, eventually using the transmission facilities of a third country;
- developing transmission links dedicated to cross-border trading; and
- implementing a wholly competitive regional market.

GMS countries have signed two MoUs that pledge close cooperation for the purposes of trading electricity and set high-level objectives for the first two stages of trading:

- **Stage 1** corresponds to the initial period when only country-to-country power transactions are possible, before a regional transmission network is established to enable power trading between any pair of member countries. During this period, trade takes place predominantly via dedicated cross-border transmission lines used by independent power providers (IPPs) located in one GMS country and sells power to a utility in a neighboring GMS country. The cross-border power trading in Stage 1 refers to opportunistic exchange of power between power utilities using the excess capacity of existing transmission lines over and above the transmission capacity required for power transfers associated with existing PPAs.
- **Stage 2** corresponds to the time when trading will be possible between any pair of GMS countries, eventually using transmission facilities of a third regional country. However, in this stage the available cross-border transmission is limited and based on surplus capacity of lines linked to PPAs.

Both stages of electricity trading rely initially on utilization of spare capacity on international interconnectors that has not been taken up by existing bilateral trades. The main distinction between the two, however, is in the potential for using the transmission assets of a **third country** through which to wheel electricity between two other countries.

Two possible scenarios can be envisaged for future trading in the GMS:

Scenario 1

- A PPA is signed between the utility or the developer who will build a generating plant.
- The plant is constructed.
- At the same time, a dedicated transmission line is built.
- Following commissioning of the generating plant and transmission line, trading commences and power flows from the generator to the purchasing utility.

Scenario 2

For full Stage 2 trading to take place in the most general conditions, the following steps would be required:

- A bilateral contract is entered into between a seller and a buyer (these may both be power utilities, or the seller could be an IPP developer, and the buyer either a utility or, ultimately, a large consumer).
- A new power plant may be constructed, though this would not necessarily be the case if trade were going to take place between two utilities using existing generation assets.
- Additional transmission infrastructure may be constructed; however, this again would not necessarily be the case. In principle, trading could utilize the transmission assets of a third-party utility; cross-border trading would therefore take place between one country and another using the transmission assets of the third country for wheeling purposes.

Since the completion of the ADB regional technical assistance (RETA 6440) on Facilitating Regional Power Trading and Environmentally Sustainable Development of Electricity Infrastructure in the Greater Mekong Subregion,[1] electricity trading in the GMS has been continually built on IPPs with dedicated transmission lines (i.e., "Scenario 1" trading). Limited progress has been made, however, toward the development of a regional electricity market that was envisaged in the ADB project. A key objective of this study is to explore why this is the case.

1.1 Existing Interconnections

Since 1992, some power generation projects have been developed with assistance from development banks and private developers. The projects have been developed for power export to neighbouring countries via dedicated cross-border interconnectors.

A comprehensive list of operational and planned future interconnectors was developed in the RETA 6440 study (Tables 1 and 2).

Table 1 shows the existing interconnections at 110 kilovolts (kV) and above within the region. These transmission lines have generally been constructed with the intention to facilitate cross-border trading of electricity from individual plants to significant load centers. These load centers are not always fully interconnected with an integrated national grid system. The ADB study reveals the limitations of

[1] ADB. 2010. *Facilitating Regional Power Trading and Environmentally Sustainable Development of Electricity Infrastructure in the Greater Mekong Subregion.* Manila. https://www.adb.org/projects/41018-012/main.

Table 1: Existing International Interconnections at 110 Kilovolts and Above in GMS Power Systems

Reference	From	To	Voltage	Capacity	IPP or Grid-Grid Interconnector
People's Republic of China–Viet Nam					
1	Guman, PRC	Lao Cai, Viet Nam	220 kV double circuit	450 MW	Grid–Grid
2	Malutang, Yunnan, PRC	Ha Giang, Viet Nam	220 kV	350 MW	Grid–Grid
3	Maomaotiao, PRC	Ha Giang, Viet Nam	110 kV double circuit	110 MW	Grid–Grid
4	Hekou, PRC	Lao Cai, Viet Nam	110 kV	70 MW	Grid–Grid
5	Fangcheng (Guangxi), PRC	Mong Cai, Viet Nam	110 kV	25 MW	Grid–Grid
Myanmar–People's Republic of China					
6	Shweli I HPP, Myanmar	Dehong, Yunnan, PRC	220 kV double circuit	600 MW (300 MW domestic use + 300 MW export to PRC)	IPP
7	Dapein I HPP, Myanmar	Dayingjiang, Yunnan, PRC	500 kV	240 MW (7MW domestic load)	IPP
8	Menglong, Myanmar	Jingyang, PRC	110 kV	N/A	Grid–Grid
Viet Nam–Cambodia					
9	Chau Doc, Viet Nam	Phnom Penh, Cambodia	220 kV (Viet Nam) 230 kV (Cambodia) double circuit	200 MW	Grid–Grid
Lao PDR–Thailand					
10	Nam Theun 2 HPP, Lao PDR	Roi Et 2 substation (via Savannakhet, Lao PDR), Thailand	500 kV double circuit	1,000 MW	IPP
11	Houayho HPP, Lao PDR	Ubon Ratchathani 2, Thailand	230 kV	120 MW	IPP
12	Theun Hinboun HPP, Lao PDR	Nakhon Phanom 2, Thailand	230 kV	440 MW	IPP
13	Nam Ngum 2 HPP, Lao PDR	Udon Thani 3, Thailand	500 kV (operated at 230 kV)[a]	615 MW, will be upgraded to 1,800 MW	IPP

continued on next page

Table 1 *continued*

Reference	From	To	Voltage	Capacity	IPP or Grid–Grid Interconnector
14	Hong Sa TPP, Lao PDR	Nan, Thailand	500 kV	1,473 MW	IPP
15	Phontong S/S (Vientiane), Lao PDR	Nongkhai (Electricity Generating Authority of Thailand), Thailand	115 kV	N/A	Grid–Grid
16	Thanaleng (Vientiane), Lao PDR	Nongkhai (Electricity Generating Authority of Thailand), Thailand	115 kV	N/A	Grid–Grid
17	Pakxan S/S (Borikhamxay), Lao PDR	Bungkan (Electricity Generating Authority of Thailand), Thailand	115 kV	N/A	Grid–Grid
18	Thakhek S/S (Khammoun), Lao PDR	Nakhon Phanom (Electricity Generating Authority of Thailand), Thailand	115 kV	N/A	Grid–Grid
19	Pakbo S/S (Savannakhet), Lao PDR	Mukdahan 2 (Electricity Generating Authority of Thailand), Thailand	115 kV	N/A	Grid–Grid
20	Bang Yo S/S (Champassak), Lao PDR	Sirinthon S/S (Electricity Generating Authority of Thailand), Thailand	115 kV	36 MW	IPP
Lao PDR–Viet Nam					
21	Xekaman 3 HPP, Lao PDR	Thanh My, Viet Nam	220 kV double circuit	248 MW	IPP
22	Xekaman 1 HPP (Hat Xan), Lao PDR	Pleiku 2, Viet Nam	220 kV	290 MW	IPP
Lao PDR–People's Republic of China					
23	Namo (Oudomxai), Lao PDR	Meng La, PRC	115 kV	60 MW	Grid–Grid
Thailand–Cambodia					
24	Aranyaprathet, Thailand	Banteay Meanchey, Cambodia	115 kV	100 MW[b]	Grid–Grid

HPP = hydropower plant, IPP = independent power producer, kV = kilovolt, Lao PDR = Lao People's Democratic Republic, MW = megawatt, N/A = not available, PRC = People's Republic of China, S/S = substation.

[a] When there will be a new connection from Nam Niep I, after 2019, it will be operated in 500 kV.
[b] EGAT. 2014. *Development of Cross – Border Trade between Thailand and Neighboring Countries*. February.

Sources: ADB. 2016. *Greater Mekong Subregion: Energy Sector Assessment, Strategy, and Road Map*. Manila. June; Regional Power Trade Coordination Committee. 2016. *Viet Nam Country Report*. EVN NLDC. December; Regional Power Trade Coordination Committee. 2016. *PRC Country Report*. December; *Greater Mekong Subregion Regional Investment Framework Implementation Plan: Mid-Term Review and Revised Regional Investment Framework Implementation Plan 2020*. December 2016; Regional Power Trade Coordination Committee. 2017. *Myanmar Country Presentation*. RPTCC-23. December; Regional Power Trade Coordination Committee. 2016. *Thailand Country Report*. December; Annex to the *Regional Investment Framework 2022: Project Pipeline, Greater Mekong Subregion Economic Cooperation Program*. September 2017; Regional Power Trade Coordination Committee. 2017. *Lao PDR Country Presentation*. RPTCC-23. December; Regional Power Trade Coordination Committee. 2017. *Viet Nam Country Presentation*. RPTCC-23. December.

the existing interconnected regional grid system and finds that additional transmission interconnection is needed to enable full regional trade to develop. This was a major finding from the RETA 6440 study, which highlighted the limitations of the existing interconnected regional grid system.

These existing interconnections are limited in their ability to contribute to the expansion of regional power trade due to (i) their limited physical capacity and (ii) the nature of the PPAs between sellers and purchasers of the relevant power, which are understood to specify the exclusive use of the transmission assets by these schemes.

Table 2 shows the list of transmission interconnection projects that have been committed for the GMS (as of 2018).

Table 2: Committed and Planned Future Interconnections in GMS Power Systems

Reference	From	To	Voltage	Capacity	IPP or Grid-Grid Interconnector
People's Republic of China–Viet Nam					
25	Denggao, Yunnan, PRC	Ho Chi Minh, Viet Nam (via Son La, Viet Nam)	500 kV or 220 kV	Under study	Grid–Grid
People's Republic of China–Myanmar					
26	Dehong, Yunnan, PRC	Kamarnat, Myanmar (via Muse, Myanmar)	500 kV Dehong-Muse is AC Muse-Kamarnt is DC	3 GW	Grid–Grid
Cambodia–Viet Nam					
27	Stung Treng, Cambodia	Tay Ninh, Viet Nam	220 kV	207 MW	N/A
Lao PDR–Thailand					
28	Ban Lak 25, Lao PDR	Ubon Ratchathani 3, Thailand	500 kV	1,300 MW	IPP Under construction COD 2019
29	MK_Xayabuly, Lao PDR	Loei 2, Thailand	500 kV	1,220 MW	IPP Under construction COD 2019
30	Paklay, Lao PDR	Tha Li, Thailand	115 kV	N/A	Grid–Grid Under construction COD 2019
31	Ton Pheung, Lao PDR	Mae Chan, Thailand	115 kV	N/A	Grid–Grid RPTCC 21-Proposed COD 2020-2024
32	Muang Houn, Lao PDR	Nan 2, Thailand	500 kV	800 MW	Grid–Grid Planned COD 2024

continued on next page

Table 2 *continued*

Reference	From	To	Voltage	Capacity	IPP or Grid–Grid Interconnector
Lao PDR–Viet Nam					
33	Xekaman Xansay, Lao PDR	Xekaman 1, Lao PDR	110 kV	32 MW	IPP COD 2018
34	Xe Kong 1&2, Lao PDR	Viet Nam	500 kV	1,800 MW	IPP COD 2021-2022
35	Nam Xam 1&3, Lao PDR	Viet Nam	220 kV	220 MW	IPP COD 2021-2022
36	Xekaman 4 HPP, Lao PDR	Xekaman 1 HPP, Lao PDR	220 kV	80 MW	IPP COD 2022
37	Hat Xan, Lao PDR	Ple ku, Viet Nam	500 kV	N/A	Grid–Grid Under study COD 2021-2025
38	Luang Prabang, Lao PDR	Nho Quan, Viet Nam	500 kV	N/A	Planned after 2020
39	HPP Nam Mo, Lao PDR	Ban Ve, Viet Nam	220 kV	N/A	IPP – PPA in negotiation Planned after 2020
People's Republic of China–Lao PDR					
40	Ban Na, PRC	Na Mo, Lao PDR	500 kV	1 GW in the first stage, 3 GW in the future depending on Thailand's needs (line planned to be reaching Thailand)	Grid–Grid Under study COD 2021
Lao PDR–Cambodia					
41	Ban Hat, Lao PDR	Stung Treng, Cambodia	230 kV	N/A	Grid–Grid COD N/A
Lao PDR–Myanmar					
42	Ton Pheung, Lao PDR	Tachileck, Myanmar	115 kV	N/A	Grid–Grid RPTCC 21–Proposed COD 2020-2024
43	M. Long, Lao PDR	Shan State, Myanmar	230 kV	N/A	Grid–Grid Planned COD 2025

COD = commercial operation date, GW = gigawatt, HPP = hydropower plant, IPP = independent power producer, kV = kilovolt, Lao PDR = Lao People's Democratic Republic, MW = megawatt, N/A = not available, PRC = People's Republic of China, S/S = substation.

Sources: Country presentations at RPTCC 2016 and 2017, GMS ASR 2016 and Consultant's research; Regional Power Trade Coordination Committee. 2016. *PRC Country Report*. December; Regional Power Trade Coordination Committee. 2017. *Lao PDR Country Presentation*. RPTCC-23. December; Annex to the *Regional Investment Framework 2022: Project Pipeline, Greater Mekong Subregion Economic Cooperation Program*. September 2017; Regional Power Trade Coordination Committee. 2016. *Thailand Country Report*. December; Regional Power Trade Coordination Committee. 2017. *Thailand Country Presentation*. RPTCC-23. December; Regional Power Trade Coordination Committee. 2016. *Lao PDR Country Report*. December; Regional Power Trade Coordination Committee. 2017. *Viet Nam Country Presentation*. RPTCC-23. December; ADB. 2016. *Greater Mekong Subregion: Energy Sector Assessment, Strategy, and Road Map*. Manila. June.

1.2 Current Levels of Energy Trading

Table 3 shows the energy consumption and import and export figures for GMS countries in recent years, which demonstrate that of the total regional energy consumption of 1,391 terawatt hours (TWh) in 2016, 23 TWh was supplied by imports from one country to another (i.e., approximately 1.6% of the total energy demand).

Table 3: Energy Consumption, Imports, and Exports in GMS Countries

	Energy Consumption (GWh)			Imports (GWh)			Exports (GWh)		
Country	2014	2015	2016	2014	2015	2016	2014	2015	2016
Cambodia	4,152	5,341	6,264	1,531	1,249	1,244	-	-	-
PRC (CSG)	959,000	963,000	990,900	1,459	1,436	1,440	2,289	1,985	1,765
Lao PDR	4,212	4,665	5,062	1,483	1,668	691	11,936	10,824	18,017
Myanmar	13,673	15,391	17,171	-	-	-	1,431	1,405	1,311
Thailand	177,580	183,467	189,000	12,268	14,426	19,831	1,594	1,769	900
Viet Nam	144,655	164,312	182,900	2,278	2,182	2,685	1,259	1,194	1,141
TOTAL	**1,303,272**	**1,336,176**	**1,391,297**	**19,019**	**20,961**	**25,891**	**18,509**	**17,177**	**23,134**

- = not applicable, GMS = Greater Mekong Subregion, GWh = Gigawatt hours, Lao PDR = Lao People's Democratic Republic, PRC (CSG) = People's Republic of China, China Southern Power Grid system.

Sources: Country presentations, December 2017; and Electricity Generating Authority of Thailand annual reports.

1.3 Problem Statement

The statistics shown in Table 3 demonstrate the key issues that require investigation:

- Why is the current level of power interchange so low despite the progress made in signing intergovernmental MoUs and completing detailed studies on future power system interconnection and market design?
- What are the key barriers that prevent a greater uptake of regional power trading?
- What pragmatic solutions are required to overcome the observed barriers?

2 Barriers to Cross-Border Trade

A series of core issues affecting the development of regional power trade in the Greater Mekong Subregion (GMS) have been identified, from discussions with stakeholders in the countries themselves over a 2-year period.

The issues identified fall under several key themes:

- **Partial visibility of trading benefits** to some or all parties, recognizing the developments needed to enable utilities to assess the scale of the benefits that could arise from importing electricity from outside their own countries
- **Regulatory and commercial issues** covering the issues that need to be addressed so that utilities and independent power providers (IPPs) can gain access to a GMS power system and enter into contracts for the sale of power to neighbouring utilities
- **Policy issues** in areas such as power sector restructuring and regulatory reform, which have the potential to restrict regional trading
- **Training and capacity building**, focusing on the most important requirements for filling any gaps in the knowledge and understanding of utility staff who are involved in the assessment, negotiation, and operation of regional trading

To date, there has been limited progress in developing any coordinated approach to regional planning of interconnectors in the GMS. Thus, to facilitate greater cooperation between GMS countries in developing regional trading, the governments signed a memorandum of understanding (MoU) in December 2012 in which they committed to develop a Regional Power Coordination Centre (RPCC).[2] The RPCC would act as a coordinating body for the development of policies on regional power trading and would play a facilitating role in enabling trading to take place effectively. Progress toward implementation has been limited but the principle is clearly established. Currently, each country undertakes its own power development planning process, but a more collaborative process is required to assess the benefits of interconnection. The ADB study on *Facilitating Regional Power Trading and Environmentally Sustainable Development of Electricity Infrastructure in the Greater Mekong Subregion* identified a range of potential future interconnector projects, and progress was made toward the creation of an integrated regional modelling database. Initial training was provided in the use of the OPTGEN modelling tool to enable the utilities to develop a regional plan for interconnection. However, this model has not been widely adopted, and there has been little progress on a coordinated effort by regional power utilities or regulatory bodies to overcome this problem. Furthermore, there is no obvious regional body currently empowered to develop such plans.

[2] The Inter-Governmental MoU for the Establishment of the Regional Power Coordination Centre in the Greater Mekong Subregion was signed in Nanning, People's Republic of China (PRC), 12 December 2012.

At present, the Regional Power Trade Coordination Committee (RPTCC) is the body with the most clearly defined remit for achieving cooperation and collaboration between regulators and power utilities in the GMS. The two subcommittees of the RPTCC—the Working Group on Regulatory Issues and the Working Group on Performance Standards and Grid Codes (WGPG)—are already working to identify common planning standards. The WGPG, through the parallel technical workstream on the ADB project Harmonizing the Greater Mekong Subregion Power Systems to Facilitate Regional Power Trade, is looking into the creation and development of a regional transmission planning database.

Promoting greater focus on the potential benefits of regional trading, requires an **integrated approach to regional power sector planning.** This should include greater collaboration to ensure that the benefits of importing and exporting electricity are fully visible to power sector players.

A major regulatory and commercial issues that can hinder increased regional power trade is the absence of any common model or shared market platform to enable trades to be negotiated efficiently. There is currently no common platform for short-term electricity trades to develop, so negotiating bespoke power purchase agreements (PPAs) is the only option available to potential importers and exporters of power.

Because of the varying degrees of unbundling the electricity sectors in GMS countries, there is no defined model for identifying potential trading parties. Power utilities or IPPs seeking to sell electricity to neighbouring countries must first identify the means of entering the electricity market to trade via an interconnector, which involves several stages, including

- negotiating access to the interconnector;
- negotiating applicable fees;
- gaining physical access to the national transmission network by independent power producers (IPPs);
- identifying a trading counterparty;
- negotiating a PPA;
- agreeing on the commissioning and other practical arrangements with the host power utility;
- agreeing on metering configurations and meter reading arrangements; and
- agreeing on the financial settlement processes.

Many of these requirements are encapsulated in the concept of **open access**, to enable generators to use the transmission assets of their host national power utility to wheel power to the national border for export purposes. Open access to transmission networks is a key requirement for independent electricity trading parties (i.e., businesses that are separate from the owners of national transmission networks) to trade electricity either with (i) customers within the national network directly, or (ii) power utilities or large consumers connected to the networks of neighbouring countries.

Open access is not essential if power trade are restricted to vertically integrated power utilities trading with one another. However, for the widest development of regional trading to take place, particularly for the expansion of the activities of IPPs—some of which are already trading successfully in the international arena—in all GMS countries should be a priority.

At present, there is little incentive for GMS countries to host trades between their neighbors and make their national systems available for **wheeling power**. Likewise, the owners of cross-border transmission lines associated with specific IPPs have no means of recovering revenues from other users of those lines.

Both problems arise from the lack of defined wheeling charge methodology in the GMS. In the absence of standard guidelines that specify the technical and commercial terms on which network assets should be made available and the charges payable, complex and protracted negotiation processes could be a potential deterrent to the parties interested in pursuing international trade.

From a **policy** perspective, the role of **national electricity regulators** in promoting regional electricity trading is important, as they have the potential to ensure that regulated power utilities give access to their networks so that IPPs can participate in regional trading. They also have the authority to ensure that vertically integrated utilities look for opportunities for power trading as part of their expansion planning processes (where the regulator and/or an associated government ministry could be responsible for approving either the planning process or the plans themselves).

A review of the status of regional regulatory bodies in the GMS indicates that the situation varies as to the degree of independence that the regulators have from national government (see Table 4).

Table 4: Current Status of Electricity Sector Regulatory Bodies in the GMS

Country	Regulator	Country	Regulator
Cambodia	Electricity Authority of Cambodia (EAC) - *an autonomous body*	Thailand	Energy Regulatory Commission - *Not fully independent*
People's Republic of China	National Energy Administration - *a government body*	Myanmar	Ministry of Electricity and Energy regulates the market. *No independent regulator*
Lao People's Democratic Republic	Ministry of Energy and Mines (MEM) has the overall responsibility for the energy industry. *No independent regulator*	Viet Nam	Electricity Regulatory Authority of Viet Nam - *a subsidiary of the Ministry of Industry and Trade*

Source: Ricardo Energy & Environment.

Within the GMS, only Cambodia currently has a regulatory institution that is fully independent from the government. The operating experience in the GMS shows that the countries already active in power exports across borders—most notably the Lao People's Democratic Republic (Lao PDR), the People's Republic of China (PRC), and Viet Nam—do not have fully independent regulatory bodies. In practice, the expansion of regional electricity trading is most affected by the extent to which

- private investors are encouraged to construct IPPs for power export purposes;
- power utilities and large consumers are enabled to purchase power from foreign sources; and
- national single buyers or vertically integrated utilities are required to purchase power from the most economical sources, irrespective of the ownership of generation assets.

These are all issues that effective regulatory functions are required to address. In practical terms, an arm's length relationship between regulators and government ministries—especially when national power utilities are under state control—helps to reassure private investors that their participation in the power sector will not be unduly influenced by political policy changes.

The most important requirement to ensure that international power trading can take place on an equitable basis, however, is for regulatory functions to be carried out independently of the interests of power utilities involved in the generation, transmission or purchase, and sale of electricity. There is no absolute requirement for fully legally independent regulatory bodies to exist as a necessary precursor to the expansion of regional power trading. Box 1 gives a definition of regulatory independence, for reference.

Box 1: Independent Regulators—A European Definition

A review of the definition of an "independent regulator" from Article 35 of the European Union's 2009 Electricity Directive states the following requirements of an independent regulator:

a. legally distinct and functionally independent from any other public or private entity
b. acts independently from any market interest
c. does not take direct instructions from any government or other entity when carrying out regulatory tasks
d. can take autonomous decisions independent of any political body
e. has autonomy in the implementation of its budget allocation
f. has senior managers appointed for fixed terms (5–7 years), renewable once

It is interesting to note that the European Union countries distinguish between the legal separation of regulatory institutions from other bodies, and the functional independence of these institutions. Regulatory bodies can demonstrate functional independence in the activities listed in b through e if they are so permitted by national governments. The emphasis in the GMS at this time should therefore be on achieving that "functional independence" that will support the role of the national regulators.

Sources: Ricardo Energy & Environment; and Directive 2009/72/EC of the European Parliament and of the Council of 13 July 2009 (concerning common rules for the internal market in electricity and repealing Directive 2003/54/EC). http://eur-lex.europa.eu/legal-content/EN/ALL/?uri=celex%3A32009L0072.

Power sector planning in GMS countries is generally performed in close cooperation with relevant government ministries that have the responsibility for final sign-off of power sector expansion plans. In the case of Viet Nam, the Electricity and Renewable Energy Authority in the Ministry of Industry and Trade (MOIT) is responsible for sector planning, while the Electricity Regulatory Authority of Viet Nam (ERAV), as a department of the same ministry, is responsible for power sector regulation. Assessing potential cross-border trading as an integral part of national power sector planning therefore requires the full engagement of planning ministries. The potential benefits of incorporating interconnection into the integrated resource planning process are currently being more fully explored under the ADB technical assistance (TA) project Integrated Resource Planning with Strategic Environmental Assessment for Sustainable Power Sector Development in the Greater Mekong Subregion.[3]

There is a question about whether **power sector restructuring** is required in each country, through the unbundling of the key functions of generation, transmission, distribution and supply to end customers, to promote open electricity trading between countries. While policy decisions in many countries have

[3] https://www.adb.org/projects/documents/integrated-resource-planning-strategic-environmental-assessment-gms-tar.

led to the liberalization of electricity markets and the unbundling of power sector entities, this has not always been essential to achieve regional power trading. Box 2 illustrates this in relation to the Southern African Power Pool. Appendix 1 provides some of the examples of the way in which regional power trade has evolved in a number of international markets.

Box 2: Southern African Power Pool and Power Sector Restructuring

The Southern African Power Pool (SAPP), described more fully in Appendix 1, is open to participation by independent power producers alongside the vertically integrated utilities and unbundled power utility businesses. The interests of all parties are protected through the governance structures of the market itself, which include an intergovernmental memorandum of understanding, an inter-utility memorandum of understanding, and an agreement between operating members.

The work of the SAPP Coordination Centre is also essential in facilitating long-term and short-term power trading. The Southern African Regional Energy Regulators' Association (RERA) seeks to promote best practice among national regulators, and this assists in the creation of a level playing field for market participants.

Source: Ricardo Energy & Environment.

Increasing the liquidity of electricity trading within the GMS requires **short-term trading rules** that enable the opportunistic use of spare capacity on international interconnectors for trades that utilize the seasonal and daily differences between power supply and demand. If the process for entering into new trades is too cumbersome, and requires lengthy negotiations between trading parties, the potential benefits of short-term trading are outweighed by the costly and time-consuming negotiation process, and the opportunity is lost.

Associated with short-term operational issues, the risks to power system security arising from any imbalance between the scheduled international trades and what actually takes place on the network need to be addressed. This requires the implementation of a **balancing mechanism** to ensure that responsibility for the costs of maintaining supply quality and security are met by the parties whose performance has had an adverse impact on the networks.

Training and capacity building are crucial in enabling regional electricity trading to develop, and the main requirements here are for both the principles of trading and the practical aspects to be explored. This includes a number of priorities:

(i) **ensuring that training in integrated resource planning techniques takes place:** This will help ensure that power utility planning staff are fully aware of the contribution that regional power trading can make to meeting national demand at the least cost. To assist this process, GMS countries are participating in the ADB TA project Integrated Resource Planning with Strategic Environmental Assessment for Sustainable Power Sector Development in the Greater Mekong Subregion. This project seeks to identify regional and international best practices in integrated resource planning methods and facilitate capacity building of the utilities and planning institutions in these areas.

(ii) **assisting utilities in evaluating the potential for long and short-term trades, taking account of the full range of costs to which they will be exposed:** This should include
- training in the technical and financial evaluation of potential trades, and
- training in the negotiation of PPAs for long-term bilateral trades and short-term trading (here, guidance in the development of pro-forma contracts may be required).

(iii) **opportunities for direct learning through study tours to regional electricity markets:** The Southern African Power Pool (SAPP), the West African Power Pool (WAPP), and the Nordic market (Nord Pool Spot) can offer valuable learning for the GMS as regional trading evolves.

(iv) **closer linkages with the Association of Southeast Asian Nations (ASEAN):** This offers learning opportunities from regional projects, such as the Lao PDR–Thailand–Malaysia–Singapore Power Integration Project (Appendix 2), and enables wide sharing of best practices.

3 Priorities for Increasing Regional Electricity Trading

From the evaluation of issues described above, several clear themes have emerged, and these will require attention if electricity trading across the GMS is to develop in practical ways. The recommendations are described in more detail in the later chapters of this document, but they are also summarized here.

3.1 Open Access Arrangements

Open access can be defined as the arrangements required to give access to an electricity transmission network to parties other than the owners of the network itself, for the purposes of generating or consuming power. Most commonly in the definition of electricity trading arrangements, it refers to the access given by either an independent system operator or a transmission owner to the network under its control, typically to an independent power producer (IPP) for the purposes of selling electricity to a customer who, again, is not the owner of the network.

In the case of a vertically integrated electricity utility that undertakes generation, transmission, and distribution and supply of electricity, Open Access would give rights to a non-utility participant to construct a generating plant and to be able to connect this to the transmission network.

Open access requires a series of **regulatory, technical,** and **commercial** measures ensure that system operators, transmission owners, and IPPs have achieved several key objectives:

(i) the ability for the system operator to operate the transmission network safely and reliably, without jeopardizing supplies to other network users

(ii) the right of the IPP to be and remain connected to the network, all the while it complies with a core set of technical conditions (typically defined in a grid code, or equivalent); and

(iii) the right of the IPP to use the transmission system for exporting power from its generating facilities to:

   a. an electricity retailer or distribution/supply business;
   b. one or more large consumer(s), who may be connected at transmission or distribution voltage levels; or
   c. a neighbouring country, using its host country transmission network to transport power to the border, to access an interconnector. In the context of enhanced power trading in the GMS, this case is particularly relevant.

Open access provisions in the GMS also extend to the issues of who has access to existing and future **international interconnectors** and how this access can be achieved. At present, many of the international interconnections are associated with specific IPPs, under the "Stage 1" electricity trading model referred to earlier. Regulatory and commercial provisions are required to ensure that future IPPs or other network users can gain access to the spare capacity on these assets for the purposes of exporting power to neighbouring countries.

3.2 Wheeling Charges

Wheeling charges are required for international trading in the GMS to support two types of trade:

- international power trades taking place under **long-term bilateral contracts**; and
- **short-term trades** taking place over a period from months down to hours ahead of real time.

The overall tariffs for energy exchanges will be governed by bilateral contracts or short-term trading rules. Reference will, however, be required in the bilateral contracts and short-term trading rules to the payment of wheeling charges. Arrangements will be needed to ensure that the payments are channelled to the appropriate national system operators who are responsible for the networks and/or interconnectors providing the wheeling services.

The wheeling charges require a methodology to recover payments related to the fixed and variable costs of providing transmission wheeling assets. These payments should include

- a contribution to the **capital costs** of the assets and the recovery of the costs of **depreciation**,
- the recovery of costs associated with **operation and maintenance (O&M)** of the transmission networks, and
- the costs of **losses** occurring on the transmission systems as a result of wheeling transactions.

The core principles of wheeling charges are to

- **promote efficiency;**
- **recover costs;**
- **be transparent, fair, and predictable;** and
- **be nondiscriminatory.**

A number of cost components can be recovered through well-designed wheeling charges, including:

- **capital costs** of the network plant and equipment,
- **O&M costs**, and
- **transmission losses** specifically associated with wheeling trades.

There are trade-offs between economic efficiency and the complexity of the charging methodologies. International electricity markets have developed a range of charging methods that cover the above cost components with varying degrees of sophistication. The GMS should adopt a methodology to allocate costs to electricity trading parties based on the power flows that they impose on transmission assets, and the resulting share of the capacity of those assets used for international trade.

3.3 Short-Term Trading Rules

To enable trading to take place over a period from a few hours to months ahead, several components of an overall methodology are required. These comprise

- a method for assessing the available transfer capacity on interconnectors, after taking account of long-term bilateral trades to ensure that short-term trading is physically possible;
- a simplified trading mechanism for proposing short-term bilateral contracts and entering into the associated commercial transactions; and
- simplified metering and settlement processes for settling contracted quantities.

Scenario 1 Trading

In the case of simple trading taking place between an IPP and a power utility over a dedicated transmission line, the potential for short- or long-term utilization of the line for additional trade will be dominated by the available capacity on the interconnector itself and in the network of the recipient utility (i.e., on the line IPP-transmission system operator (TSO) TSO (Figure 1) and within the network of the utility itself). The TSO has responsibilities both as the owner and operator of transmission assets.

The spare transmission capacity can be calculated easily, using the information on thermal and voltage constraints on the dedicated interconnector and on the capacities of the lines immediately adjacent to the point at which the IPP generation enters the TSO's network. The calculation would use conventional power flow analysis.

Figure 1: Simple Interconnection Used in Scenario 1 Trading

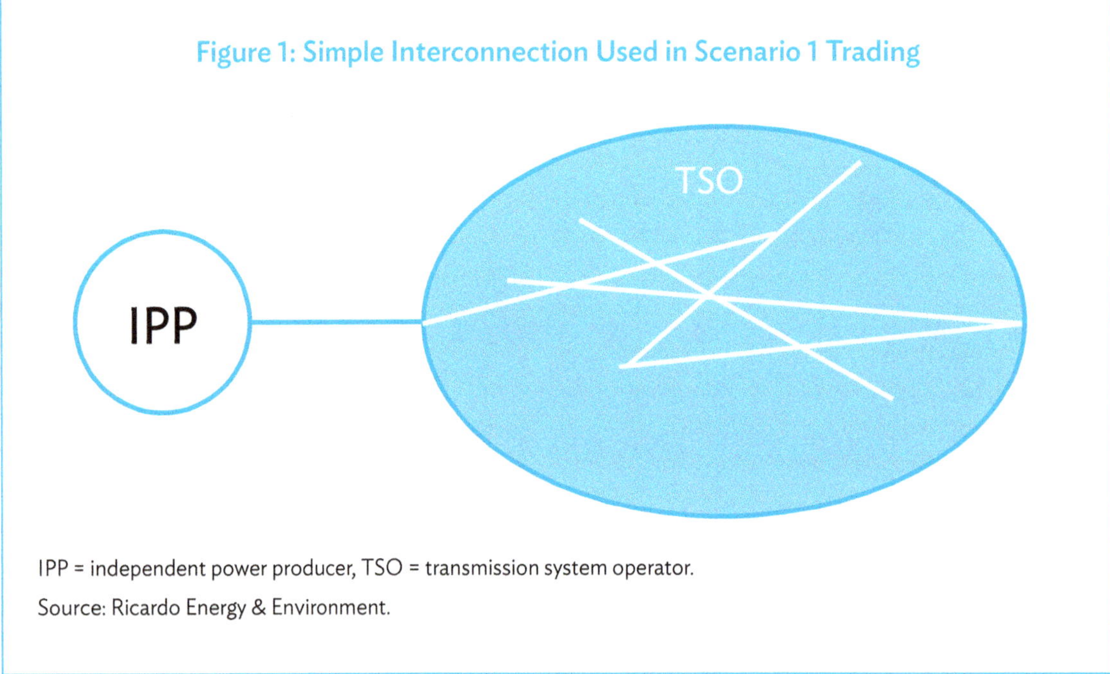

IPP = independent power producer, TSO = transmission system operator.

Source: Ricardo Energy & Environment.

Scenario 2 Trading

Determining the availability of transmission capacity to facilitate Stage 2 trading, requires a requires a methodology to assess the available transfer capability (ATC) within a wheeling country (Figure 2).

ATC is typically defined with reference to the total transfer capability (TTC) on an interconnection and the need for a transfer reliability margin (TRM) on the interconnector, to cater to the power flow needed between systems in contingency situations.

Cross-border trading in the GMS has already commenced using power purchase agreements (PPAs) between IPPs and utilities. These complex multi-annual contracts are designed to support the long-term viability of individual power projects. Currently, trading is limited to Scenario 1 trades under long-term PPAs using dedicated transmission assets.

To facilitate trading on a more flexible basis, however, an additional contracting structure between

- generators and power utilities or single buyers,
- utility and utility,
- utility and large consumer, or
- generator and large consumer.

A set of contracts could therefore be envisaged that would cover the above combinations, and which would ideally facilitate bilateral trading over time frames from year-ahead to on-the-day (e.g., one hour before real time). However, for intra-day trading to be possible, this would have to be fully automated and should enable buyers and seller to trade anytime of the day or night. Developing a trading platform to enable this should be an aspiration for the GMS. However, this is not proposed as an immediate next step.

Figure 2: Trading via an Interconnection through a Third-Party Network

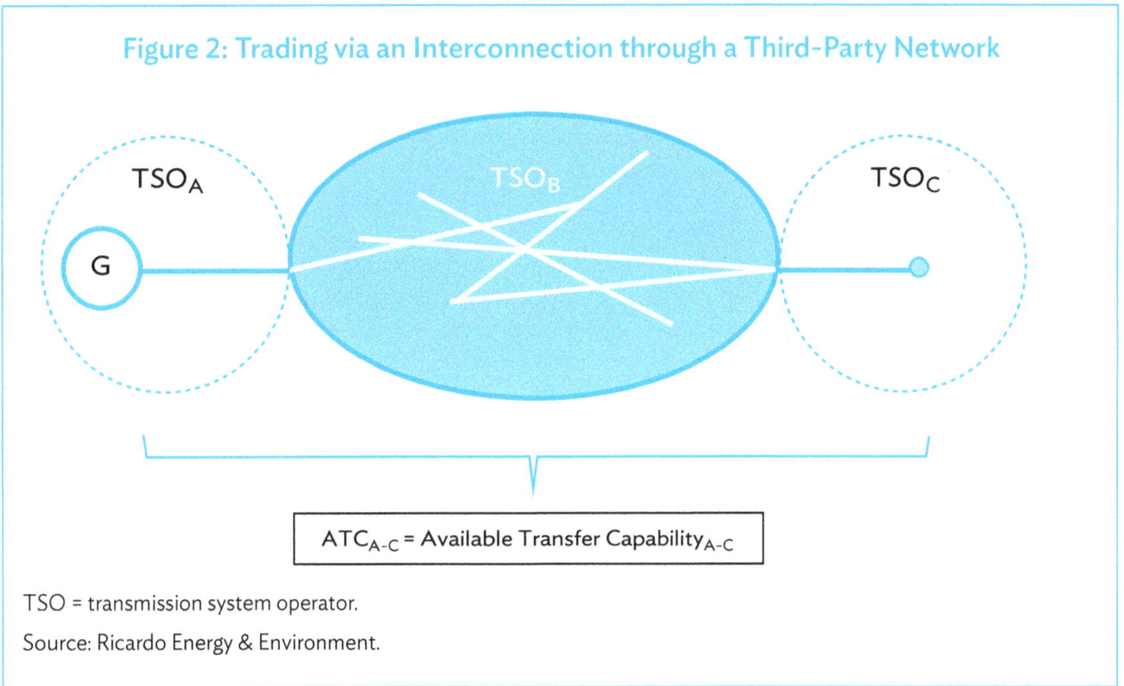

TSO = transmission system operator.

Source: Ricardo Energy & Environment.

The highest priority for short-term trading is to enable seasonal surpluses in one country to be sold to another country, and the purchase of power when there are unforeseen shortages. Trading should therefore be permitted down to the day before real time to maximize the benefits of these potential trades. This would be achievable using a bulletin-board type approach to match willing buyers and willing sellers, and could be achieved within the current environment in which vertically integrated utilities and single buyer organizations are the focal point for electricity trading. It would not require major changes to either the structure of the power sector in GMS countries or the rollout of sophisticated power trading tools.

3.4 Balancing Mechanism

Imbalances that arise between scheduled interchanges and what actually happens in practice need to be settled. This ensures that utilities whose networks are providing balancing energy are not left with a financial deficit.

Two options exist for settling imbalances:

- **"in-kind"** repayment of energy at times of day and seasons of the year that correspond to those when the imbalance occurred. This will help ensure that the energy replaced has approximately the same value to the utility that provided the balancing service as the energy it supplied and
- **a cash-based** settlement mechanism, based on an understanding of which power plant(s) provided the balancing service and, therefore, the cost of the energy supplied.

"In-kind" settlement of imbalances is likely to be the most effective way forward for the GMS in the short term; however, there could be a risk that the same TSOs repeatedly rely on energy from others unless a system of penalties is in place.

In its most sophisticated form, the second option may involve the development of a market for balancing services. This would give the opportunity for potential service providers to offer prices and quantities of energy that would be called upon by a combination of automatic and manual processes, to maintain system balance. Payments would then be made based on the knowledge of which resources are required to balance the network following any given event.

It is proposed that the "in-kind" repayment is adopted as the standard approach until all parties agree with the principles, timeline, and calculation formulae of the cash-based settlement mechanism. Under this arrangement, cash-based settlement should only be used as a last resort measure in the case wherein the buyer and the seller cannot find a mutually acceptable arrangement for the imbalance to be paid back in-kind. See Appendix 3 for a review of international practice in the settlement of imbalances.

4 Open Access Proposals

4.1 Open Access Principles for the GMS

The starting point for developing open access in the Greater Mekong Subregion is to consider cross-border transmission assets being owned by specific independent power producers (IPPs), which are then made available to other generators. This situation arises in cases where there is spare capacity on existing cross-border transmission lines. This can happen in cases where the capacity of a line exceeds the maximum output of an IPP, due to either the conservative design assumptions or the step changes in line ratings that occur between voltages and/or conductor sizes.

Figure 3 shows the case of an IPP (IPP 1) connected to a transmission line that crosses a national border. The IPP in Country A is assumed to be selling power to a utility in Country B and using its own transmission line for the purpose. The line is dedicated to the power plant and assumed as not

Figure 3: Independent Power Purchaser Connected to Its Own Cross-Border Transmission Line

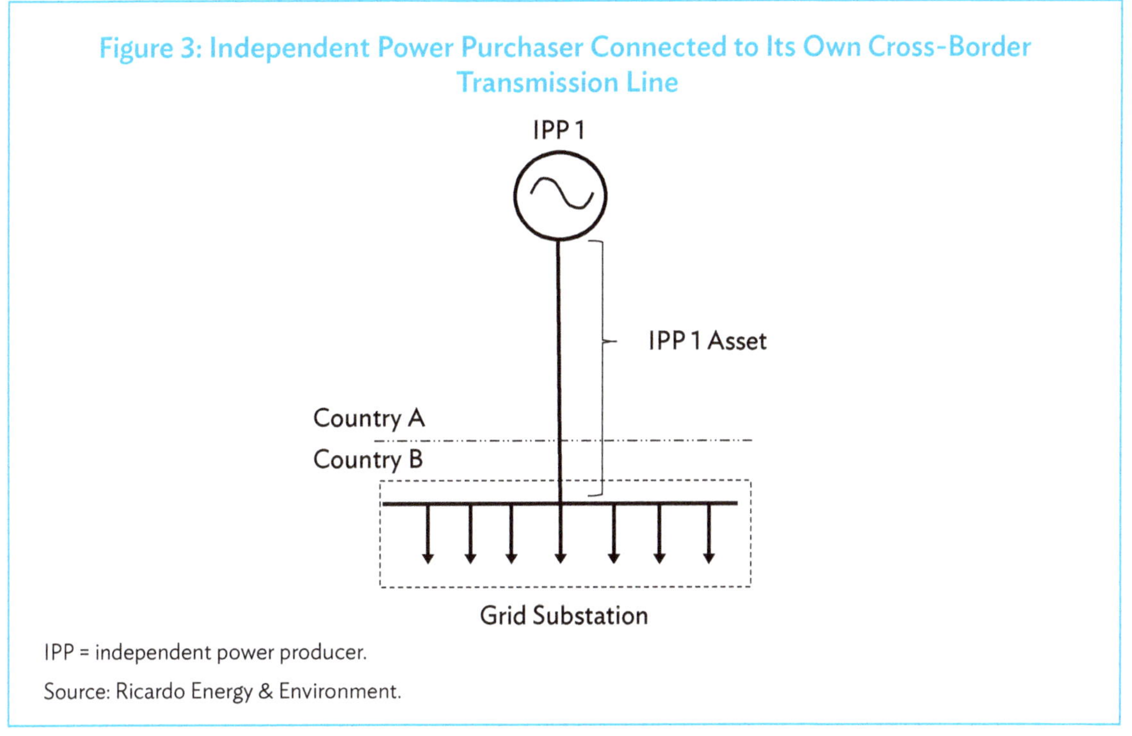

IPP = independent power producer.

Source: Ricardo Energy & Environment.

interconnected with the remainder of the network. This situation is typical of many of the hydro stations in the Lao People's Democratic Republic (Lao PDR), for example, selling electricity to the Electric Generating Authority of Thailand (EGAT) power network.

This situation is relatively straightforward when viewed from commercial and regulatory perspectives. IPP 1 requires

- a **power purchase agreement (PPA)** with the utility in Country B, or, if the power is being sold to a wholesale electricity market, the relevant market agreements to enable power trading to take place;
- a **connection and/or use of system agreement**, or equivalent, with the national TSO in Country B to ensure that it meets the technical requirements of power system operation of Country B. The terms of this agreement should include a clear definition of the interface point between IPP 1's transmission line and the system operator in Country B. Depending on whether the power from IPP 1 is purchased by the utility in Country B at the interconnection point with the transmission network in Country B, or whether the power purchaser is located remotely from the substation on the border, a national transmission use of system charge may be payable in Country B; and
- a **generation license,** or equivalent, entitling the IPP to operate its plant in Country A and to export power to Country B; the export provision could be handled in a separate **export license** in Country A.

When a second IPP (IPP 2 in the example below) seeks to connect to the cross-border transmission line, making use of the spare capacity on the line for international trading, a shared set of "wheeling assets" is created between points A and B (Figure 4). The function of these assets becomes much the same as any other transmission line in an interconnected network. They are now "shared use" assets, serving the requirements of more than one transmission user (IPP 1 and IPP 2).

Figure 4: Second IPP Connecting to the Transmission Asset of the First IPP

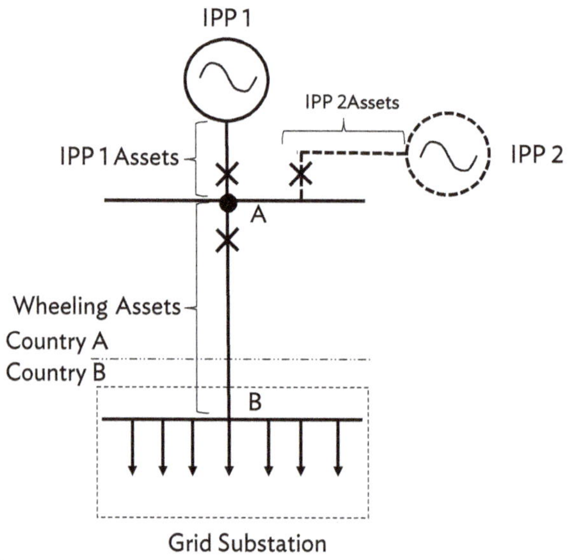

IPP = independent power producer.

Source: Ricardo Energy & Environment.

In this situation, the owner and operator of the portion of the transmission line between A and B (which may or may not be the same organization) have additional responsibilities to ensure that the line is operated and maintained in such a way that both IPP 1 and IPP 2 can gain access to the asset to transmit electricity to the border. **If IPP 1 owns the line, then it is required to grant Open Access to IPP 2, so that IPP 2 can sell its power across the border.**

In this situation, it may be desirable to follow a procedure to transfer responsibility for the wheeling asset to a national transmission company when the role of that asset changes, because it is effectively now becoming part of the main transmission network in Country A.

If control of the transmission line were to remain with IPP 1, there could be the potential for discrimination against the interests of IPP 2 (e.g., if maintenance requirements were to constrain the capacity available on the interconnector). To ensure neutrality in the operation of the transmission system, main system assets should ideally be operated by transmission companies that have no links to generators, and under the control of the national system operator. Any transmission line that is shared by more than one IPP should therefore be transferred to the system operator to become part of the main transmission network.

If the system operator forms part of a vertically integrated utility, clear regulatory provisions should be put in place governing the rights of third parties to access the main transmission network assets.

One challenge in the GMS is to increase the level of interconnection in GMS power systems.[4] Consequently, the national transmission networks may expand to give greater access to cross-border transmission lines (Figure 5).

Figure 5: Extension of Open Access Principles to the Interconnected National Network

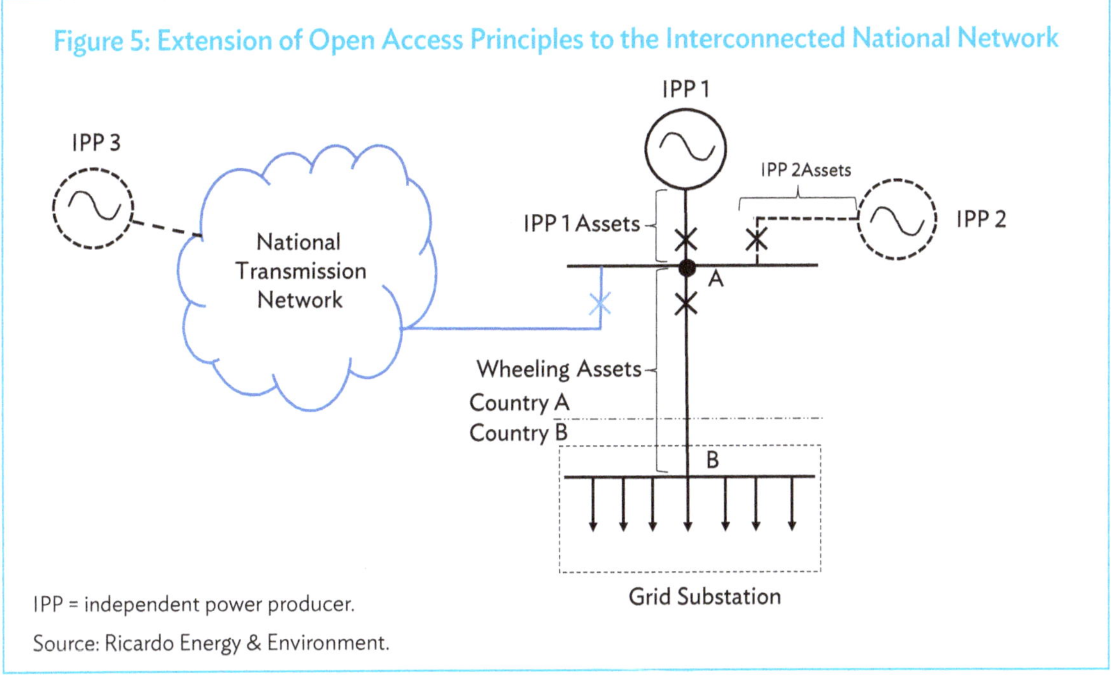

IPP = independent power producer.

Source: Ricardo Energy & Environment.

[4] ADB. 2010. *Facilitating Regional Power Trading and Environmentally Sustainable Development of Electricity Infrastructure in the Greater Mekong Subregion.* Manila. https://www.adb.org/projects/41018-012/main.

In this case, the cross-border transmission line has become interconnected with the national transmission network in Country A; and provisions are required such that if a third IPP (IPP 3 in Figure 5) seeks access to the international interconnector, it can obtain the necessary licenses and agreements with the system operator in Country A to make this possible.

4.2 Regulatory and Contractual Requirements for Open Access

The key requirements for ensuring open access in GMS countries are the following:

- **licensing arrangements** for the transmission owner and the TSO in each country, either as independent organizations or as functions within a vertically integrated utility;
- **a license obligation for transmission utilities to offer terms** to new potential generators seeking to generate electricity for domestic consumption, or to export electricity under wheeling arrangements;
- a **transmission connection agreemen**t that clearly defines the rights and obligations of generators, the transmission owner, and the TSO when a new connection is sought;
- a **transmission use of system agreement** that supports the right of the generator to be and remain connected to and energized by the national transmission network; and
- a **wheeling contract** that links the parties benefitting from the wheeling service (i.e., the exporting utility or IPP, and the importing utility/customer) and the country or countries providing the wheeling service, and sets down the technical parameters and charges associated with the wheeling service.

Both the connection agreement and the use of system agreement should cross-reference a national grid code, a regional grid code, and other technical standards that govern both the connection of generators to the transmission system and the operation of the system with IPPs connected. It is essential that both connection and operational issues are covered, if the integrity of the transmission system is to be maintained and the power system security is not to be compromised.

To develop Stage 2 cross-border trading in the GMS, wheeling arrangements need to be formalized so that the power generated in one country can be transmitted to demand in a second country through the transmission network of a third country. Thus, the transmission assets of Country B are used to transfer power generated in Country A to demand in Country C (Figure 6).

Figure 6: Power Wheeling through a Third-Party Country Network

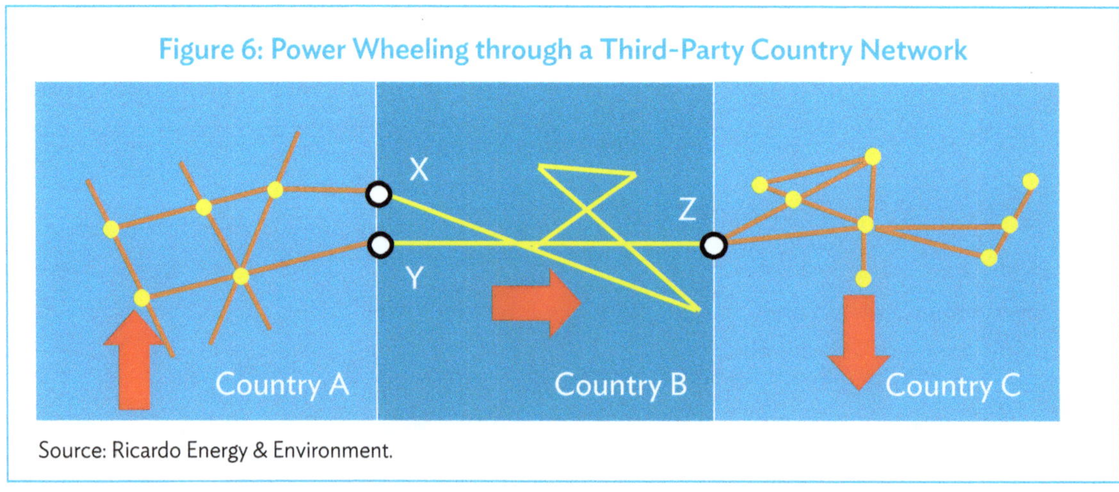

Source: Ricardo Energy & Environment.

Note that in this example

- the electricity generated in Country A could be produced by a power utility or an IPP;
- the "consumer" in Country C could be a specific industrial customer or a power utility;
- Country B is the provider of wheeling services. It makes its entire interconnected network available for the purposes of wheeling power from Country A to Country C; and
- the additional power flow in the system will be determined by the overall system connectivity.

To enable the technical and commercial arrangements to be put in place to support wheeling, the **Wheeling Contract** should specify the **wheeling capacity** needed and the **wheeling charges** that will be levied on the transaction by the system operator in Country B. Cross references should be specified in the relevant **quality of supply standards or grid code** requirements to be complied with by all parties.

Either the wheeling contract or the PPA needs also to cover

- arrangements for dealing with **transmission losses** that arise from the wheeling transaction;
- the need for **balancing arrangements** to ensure that the TSOs are not exposed to increased costs if the wheeling transaction does not take place; and
- arrangements for covering the costs of **ancillary services**, such as reactive power and frequency response services.

4.3 Immediate Next Steps for GMS Countries

The immediate priorities for GMS countries are to (i) formalize clearly defined regulations and commercial contracts for open access and wheeling, and (ii) introduce wheeling charges that are based on a robust, cost-reflective, and transparent methodology.

To progress both objectives, it is proposed that practical examples are developed with the assistance of GMS countries, to identify the specific regulations, agreements, and charging arrangements that would be needed to support individual transactions. These should focus on several specific tasks, including

- working with GMS countries that are developing their internal open access and transmission charging arrangements to ensure that these are compatible with the requirements of regional power wheeling;
- identifying examples of specific interconnectors that have spare capacity available, and developing the regulations, agreements, and tariff arrangements to give access to third parties;
- examining the subsidy and taxation regimes that apply to power imports and exports, and highlighting relevant issues that require resolution before trading can take place; and
- developing a case of grid-to-grid trading, potentially using the transmission system of a third country for wheeling purposes, and developing the necessary charging and trading arrangements (including balancing rules) that would enable trading to proceed.

5 Methodology for Wheeling Charges

5.1 Wheeling Charge Methodology: Context

Wheeling charges are a fundamental requirement for the successful integration and operation of regional transmission networks. A wheeling charge is the price that the power network users pay to the transmission asset owners and operators so that the former can use the latter's assets. Implementing a wheeling charge that safeguards asset owners' investments while offering the best deal to energy users is critical to ensuring that the regional power network is fit for its purpose and encouraging new investment in the system.

At present, there is little incentive for Greater Mekong Subregion (GMS) countries, which are required to host trades between their neighbors, to make their national systems available for wheeling power. Existing cross-border trades mainly use interconnectors dedicated to specific power plants and take place between countries sharing a border in common. Revenues to recover the costs of these transmission lines are included under the terms of power purchase agreements (PPAs) associated with specific independent power producers, and the owners of these cross-border transmission lines have no means of recovering revenues from other users of those lines.

When electricity needs to flow across a third-party's power network, wheeling charges need to be calculated separately from the energy selling price and the mechanism provided, to enable the wheeling utility to receive the associated revenues. This is key to ensuring that in a regional trade, all participants, including the wheeling parties as well as the seller and the buyer, are treated fairly. This, in turn, promotes further collaboration and trading between member countries.

However, it is difficult to define how transmission assets should work to support different power flows and implementing a fair and effective tariff is a complex task. International experience shows that setting up a wheeling charge generally requires a balance between the absolute need to ensure full cost recovery to promote investment; the necessity to keep the method simple and easy to use (so that the tariff setting process is easily applied and replicable); and the desire to treat all network users fairly by only charging them for their actual and individual cost to the network (including the cost of losses, when applicable).

5.2 Wheeling Charge Principles

The core principles of transmission pricing are to:

- **promote efficiency** by providing appropriate price signals to generation and demand, giving incentives for appropriate investment and promoting competition. It is important to consider the link between transmission pricing and the associated electricity trading arrangements, particularly in relation to congestion charging.
- **recover costs.** Different methodologies can determine the costs to be recovered (e.g., historic costs vs. forward-looking costs). Security in cost recovery lowers the risk of network investment, and hence the cost of capital.
- **be transparent, fair, and predictable** to encourage new market participants. Ideally the methodology should be easy to explain and should be stable in the long-term, avoiding "price shocks."
- **be nondiscriminatory** (i.e., treat network users who have the same impact on the transmission network equally. For example, transmission pricing should ensure that the recovery of any residual costs (where price signals do not recover the full costs required) is allocated fairly.

Cost recovery

Some cost components can be recovered through transmission prices, including capital costs of network plant and equipment, operation and maintenance costs (O&M), losses, and congestion.

Capital costs

Historical cost approaches rely on obtaining an accurate calculation of the annuitized cost of network assets. This needs to be based on an accurate assessment of the cost of the existing network, obtained from an asset valuation. The asset costs can be modified to include an allowance for the costs of system operation and maintenance. These approaches are generally good at recovering actual system costs, although there are trade-offs at the extent to which historical costs are considered to be economically efficient.

Greater economic efficiency is gained from **"forward-looking"** pricing methodologies. These assign part or all of the costs of providing new transmission facilities to the transactions that trigger the need for investment. Only the new transmission costs caused by a new transaction are considered in calculating the transmission charge. Some methodologies use "forward-looking" concepts, which differ in their use of incremental and marginal costs and also in their definitions of the short-run and long-run.

The incremental cost of a transaction is determined by comparing the total system costs with and without the transaction. This can be very different from the marginal cost of the transaction, which is calculated by assessing the extra cost of providing an extra unit of transmission. This is due to the likelihood that a transmission system is sub-optimally designed for current patterns of use for historical reasons, and the "lumpy" nature of transmission investment, which sometimes leads to the provision of over-capacity being cost-effective.

In **short-run costing**, only operating costs are considered, with the result that it is unlikely that system prices will be allowed to rise to the levels necessary to recover the full costs of the required new investment. In a perfect market, short- and long-run costs would be identical. In practice, the presence of large fixed costs and economies of scale in transmission systems means that short-run costs (in which the network is considered to be invariant) are less than long-run costs (which include the costs of system expansion/reinforcement).

Whichever method is used for signalling capital costs to network users, there is likely to be a requirement to scale the final incomes received to meet the revenue requirements of the network company. A key issue in transmission pricing concerns the relative size of this scaling component compared with the level of revenue recovered through the application of the "pure" prices. If the scaling component becomes too significant, there is risk that the method reverts toward a flat charge that is unrelated to the use of network assets, which risks losing a significant degree of economic efficiency.

Operation and maintenance costs

O&M costs are most readily recovered by allowing a predetermined margin on the capital costs of equipment to cover an appropriate amount on an annual basis the O&M costs of each asset. Annual allowances vary from utility to utility, but typical figures ranging from 2% to 5% of the capital cost per annum are applied to cover O&M costs for the system as a whole. This must be sufficient to cover the costs of operating the centralized control functions within the transmission system operator (TSO) business, as well as the maintenance requirements of the individual assets themselves.

Network losses

In principle, the cost of transmission losses can be included in the costs recovered by the transmission pricing methodology, although this depends on understanding the actual costs to which TSOs are exposed. Many international market models leave the allocation of losses for the electricity market to resolve through the adjustment of metered quantities in the settlement process. Key considerations here are (i) the mechanism by which the costs of losses are recovered, and (ii) how the transmission utility is incentivized to reduce losses (e.g., by making investments in low-loss transformers and carefully optimizing conductor sizes.

Particular attention to losses is required in the design of a wheeling charge methodology, to ensure that only those *incremental* losses associated with the impact of specific wheeling trades on the network are taken into consideration.

5.3 Historic Cost Methodologies

This section gives an overview of alternative transmission pricing methodologies and the strengths and weaknesses of the alternative approaches.

Postage Stamp

The postage stamp approach is generally regarded as the simplest to implement. The methodology allocates system costs between users on the basis of their share of total peak load on the system. It therefore results in a flat transmission charge per unit of demand equal to the total transmission costs divided by peak load. The postage stamp method is often supported with reference to the fact that, in power transactions, electrons do not actually travel from the seller to the buyer, and the system is operated on an integrated basis.

This transmission charge methodology has some advantages:

- **Full historic cost recovery is ensured**. The postage stamp method allows investors to recover their investment costs and solves the problem of under-recovery of investment costs that can become apparent in nodal pricing approaches.
- The system results in **a clear, simple, and stable** transmission charge as each consumer pays the same charge, regardless of location. Also, as the peak load is likely to increase at a relatively moderate pace in most cases, the charge is largely invariant with time.
- Postage stamp pricing is most justified in systems in which there are **few constraints and load and generators are fairly equally spaced**. In such systems, bulk power transmission costs do not significantly increase with the distance between buyers and sellers.

However, the postage stamp method does suffer from a some significant problems:

- The methodology does not consider the actual utilization of the system, and therefore does not create the correct incentives for system users. This can result in serious efficiency concerns, as users are not liable for the full costs of their actions. Transactions that impose costs on the network that outweigh their benefits may still take place, as the parties to the transaction face only a small part of the extra transmission cost.
- Although users face the same transmission tariff, the postage stamp methodology discriminates against low-cost transmission users in favor of higher-cost users. In effect, those parties engaging in high-cost transmission deals are subsidized by those who—for instance because they utilize only a small part of the network—create a smaller fraction of the transmission costs. This provides incentives for low-cost users to bypass the existing transmission network.

Contract Paths

Under the contract path methodology, a specific path is agreed for an individual wheeling transaction between two points. This “contract path” does not take account of the actual path of the power flow that would occur, but rather is based on calculations related to an assumed set of assets used by the transaction. A share of the asset costs, including the costs of new investment along the contract path, is allocated to the wheeling customer in proportion to its use.

The contract path methodology does create some benefits. The most notable of these benefits are similar to those of the postage stamp method:

- **Full cost recovery is possible** as all asset costs along the contract path are considered, including the costs of new assets if they are required. This allows investors to benefit fully from their actions, thus encouraging an efficient level of investment.
- The system creates a **simple and stable** pricing regime, and it is easy to implement.
- Relative to the postage stamp methodology, the contract path approach provides an **improved ability to signal the costs of decisions** by individual users.

However, similar to the postage stamp method, the contract path methodology ignores the actual system operation and disregards the actual power flows that are imposed on each network asset as a result of the wheeling transaction. It also disregards any congestion issues that may arise on the system. An energy transaction will in practice affect all assets on the transmission system, not just those along the contract path. This may lead to the need to invest in areas of the system that are not on the contract path at all. Therefore, the use of a contract path approach is low in economic efficiency, as well as potentially discriminating between users, depending on the way in which the contract path is identified.

Megawatt-kilometer, Distance-Based

This methodology is an extension of the concept behind the postage stamp and contract path approaches. The distance travelled by the energy transmitted under a specific transaction is either determined on a "straight-line" basis between the points of entry and exit to the network, or on a contract path approach. The megawatt-kilometer (MW-km) of the transaction is then determined (i.e., the product of the MW power flow associated with the transaction and the distance travelled in km on the system) and the ratio of this to the total system (i.e., MW-km) is calculated. This ratio is then used to determine the cost of the transaction.

As an enhancement of the postage stamp method, the distance-based methodology possesses the majority of the same advantages. The total cost of all transmission activities includes fixed and variable costs, allowing investors to fully recover their costs, thus providing efficient investment incentives. Also, the relatively simple and clear nature of the methodology makes it easy both for the users to understand the system of transmission prices and for the method to be implemented.

However, as with the previous methodologies, the actual operation and costs incurred in the system are not fully considered. Although the distance between delivery and receipt does provide some indication of actual use of the system, it still fails to take account of the impact of Kirchoff's Law, which states that electricity will follow the path of least resistance. Thus, the distance-based approach does not provide the correct economic signals to users, leading to reduced allocative and dynamic efficiency and discrimination between users.

Megawatt-kilometer, Load Flow-Based

The load flow-based MW-km methodology reflects to a better extent the actual usage of the power system. Transmission prices are determined in relation to the proportion of the transmission system used by individual transactions, as determined by load-flow studies.

A power flow model is used to calculate the flow caused by the transaction on each circuit of the transmission system. The ratio of the power flow due to the transaction and the circuit capacity is then determined. This ratio is multiplied by the circuit cost to obtain a cost for the transaction on each circuit. The share of the total system costs for the transaction is the sum of the costs for each circuit. The method is referred to as "MW-km" because the circuit cost will broadly be proportional to the length of the overhead line or cable route and the power flow imposed on the network.

The relatively simple and clear calculation of transmission charges using this method increases the degree of transparency of charges. In addition, users face prices that more closely relate to their use of the network and, hence, the costs they impose on the network. This results in decreased discrimination between users and increased allocative efficiency. However, this approach still fails to signal the costs of future investment caused by individual users' decisions, based on the recovery of historic costs. Additionally, it is expected that the total power flows on each line or cable are less than the circuit capacity; hence, not all the transmission system capital costs can be recovered. If congestion occurs due to the transactions, this will be observed from the results of the load flow; a separate methodology to address congestion can be considered.

Refinements to this method include

- replacing the circuit capacities with the sum of the total power flow caused by all transactions to fully recover the costs of network assets; and
- taking account of the direction of the flow, so that if the flow on any particular line arising from the transaction is in the opposite direction of the net flow, then the transaction is not charged with the cost of that asset. The transaction imposes a net flow reduction for the asset, which is beneficial to the system.

5.4 Forward-Looking Methodologies

Short-Run Pricing

Short-run forward pricing methodologies include short-run incremental cost (SRIC) pricing and short-run marginal cost (SRMC) pricing. Within the SRIC methodology, all operating costs associated with the whole new transmission transaction are allocated to that transaction. This differs from the marginal cost methodology in that the SRMC method identifies the operating cost of a marginal unit of additional transmission use (i.e., the increase in losses and congestion costs) (see *Capital costs* under Section 5.2).

Under the SRIC approach, costs are calculated using a model of optimal power flows. On the other hand, to estimate the SRMC, the marginal operating cost of an extra 1 MW of power is calculated at all points of delivery and receipt. This is then multiplied by the size of the transaction to provide SRMCs.

Despite the different methods of calculation, the advantages and disadvantages of the two methods are very similar. In using the pricing methods, a number of common concerns must be addressed:

- It is difficult to accurately evaluate the operating costs of a single transaction when multiple transactions occur simultaneously, and an assessment has to be made about which investment cost relates to which individual transaction.
- The use of SRIC methodology requires the forecasting of future operating costs. Such forecasts clearly become decreasingly accurate as the time horizon increases.
- The short-term nature of pricing methodology leads to two issues: (i) it is likely that transmission prices based on the methods will be volatile, and (ii) the use of SRMC/SRIC approaches may lead to under-recovery of investment costs.

In addition, there are some additional disadvantages in using the SRMC process:

- If the individual transaction is very large in relation to the transmission system load, then the SRMC price may not be an accurate estimate of the actual extra costs imposed by the transaction, as they fail to capture additional system reinforcement costs imposed.
- Once any investment is made, the future SRMC prices will fall, reducing the potential for the network owner to fully recover these costs.

However, with these transmission pricing methodologies, the transmission price for a transaction is approximately equal to the actual cost placed upon the network due to the transaction, thus promoting efficiency in the recovery of the transmission system cost.

Long-Run Pricing

Long-run, forward-pricing methodologies include long-run incremental cost (LRIC) and long-run marginal cost (LRMC). The LRIC methodology is similar to that of the SRIC; however, in LRIC, both operating and investment costs are considered. Investment costs are estimated from the change caused in long-term investment plans due to individual transaction.

The LRMC method differs from SRMC methodology only in the use of marginal investment costs as well as marginal operating costs to determine transmission costs. To calculate the extra investment costs, future transmission expansion projects are costed. This cost is then divided by the size of new planned transmission transactions to calculate the marginal investment cost.

The advantages and disadvantages of LRIC and LRMC pricing are almost identical. Estimating the investment costs and evaluating the costs caused by individual transactions can be difficult. Multiple transactions occurring simultaneously create problems in assessing which investment cost relates to which individual transaction, and, therefore the extent to which users should contribute to new investments. This is particularly so when new beneficiaries connect to the system at a later date. The sensitivity of future investment programs to assumptions on future system use means that transmission prices can be rather unstable. There may also be concerns over double-counting of investment requirements, in that these are driven by congestion costs that are also captured in LRMC pricing through the inclusion of operating costs.

Despite these problems, there are advantages apparent under the long-run methodologies that are not apparent with short-run methods:

- Users face the full long-term costs of their actions, including the costs of new investments.
- Prices are more stable in the long-run pricing, allowing users to more easily engage in long-term contracts.

5.5 Nodal Pricing

The nodal pricing methodology, where a node can be any point in the network, can be seen as the economically "ideal" transmission pricing system as prices are calculated to accurately reflect the costs imposed on the system by any transaction. The difference in charges at each node on the system (which is equal to the transmission charge between these nodes) is set on the basis of the marginal cost of losses and congestion at that node (i.e., the cost of injecting one additional unit of energy at that node). Nodal prices obviate the issue of which assets are used for wheeling purposes by not defining the path followed by flows between nodes. Instead, prices are set on the basis of the marginal impact on the system as a whole.

The nodal methodology provides for any busbar, or node, on the network, a pricing signal relative to any other node. For nodes located in areas with surplus generation, there will be a comparatively high cost for additional generation; conversely for nodes located in areas with a deficit of generation, the price for adding load will be high. Parties considering electricity trading can obtain an indication of the price of power transfers between nodes on the network. Similarly, potential investors in transmission lines can obtain an indication of the returns they might make on investments in different parts of the network.

In its simplest form, the optimal dispatch problem involves

- minimizing, at each node, the cost of supply; while
- limiting line flows to their capacity limits; and
- ensuring that total demand equals total supply.

In this simple model, the nodal pricing system solves the dispatch problem in a decentralized market by ensuring that the marginal cost at all supplying nodes is equal to the marginal benefit at all consuming nodes. This results in users consuming electricity up to the point where their marginal value of power is equal to the marginal cost of supply—the nodal price—ensuring that both allocative and dynamic efficiency are maximized.

Nodal pricing can lead to optimal dispatch in a more complex model incorporating transmission losses and congestion costs. Each nodal price is equal to the cost of providing an extra unit of electricity to the node, including costs of losses and congestion. Thus, efficiency is still maximized within the more complex model. The methodology results in transmission charges being variable by time and location. Individual nodal prices can change instantaneously to allow for changes in supply and demand, as well as being dependent on distance from generation.

Although nodal pricing methodology leads to maximum efficiency benefits, some issues have resulted in the system being rarely adopted in practice for network pricing alone:

- It is probable that nodal pricing will result in under-recovery of fixed costs, as pricing is a function of marginal costs. This does not allow for the recovery of the significant existing fixed costs that characterize transmission networks, which lead to average total costs exceeding short-run marginal costs. For these costs to be more fully recovered, it is necessary to move to a system of "second-best" pricing in which economic efficiency is sacrificed for prices that allow the network operator to recover all costs, including variable and fixed costs.
- To set the prices, the TSO would require constant real-time information about all loads, generators, bids, and the condition of all equipment. Prices would not only vary over different nodes, but also over time as elements such as supply, demand, and transmission constraints change. This creates significant instability and complexity in implementation, requiring advanced information technology and communications, often resulting in countries adopting different pricing systems or simplifications of full nodal pricing.

5.6 The Trade-Off Between Complexity and Efficiency

There is a trade-off between the computational complexity of the methods outlined above and the efficiency with which they reflect the use of transmission assets. Complexity in a calculation process tends to work against the transparency of the approach and the ease with which it can be understood by a nonspecialist. Overcomplicating the methodology should be avoided, bearing in mind the importance of wheeling charges in enabling future investors in IPPs and transmission infrastructure to understand the costs to which they are exposed and the way in which these are recovered. At the same time, for investors to have confidence in the methodology, they must see that the charges calculated are fully cost-reflective and do not discriminate against users of the transmission networks.

A qualitative review examines the methods based on their efficiency and complexity (Figure 7). This assessment can be helpful in guiding the development of an initial approach, which, can evolve as experience in applying network charges grows (see Section 5.7).

Figure 7: Indicative Trade-Off between Complexity and Efficiency in Alternative Transmission Pricing Methods

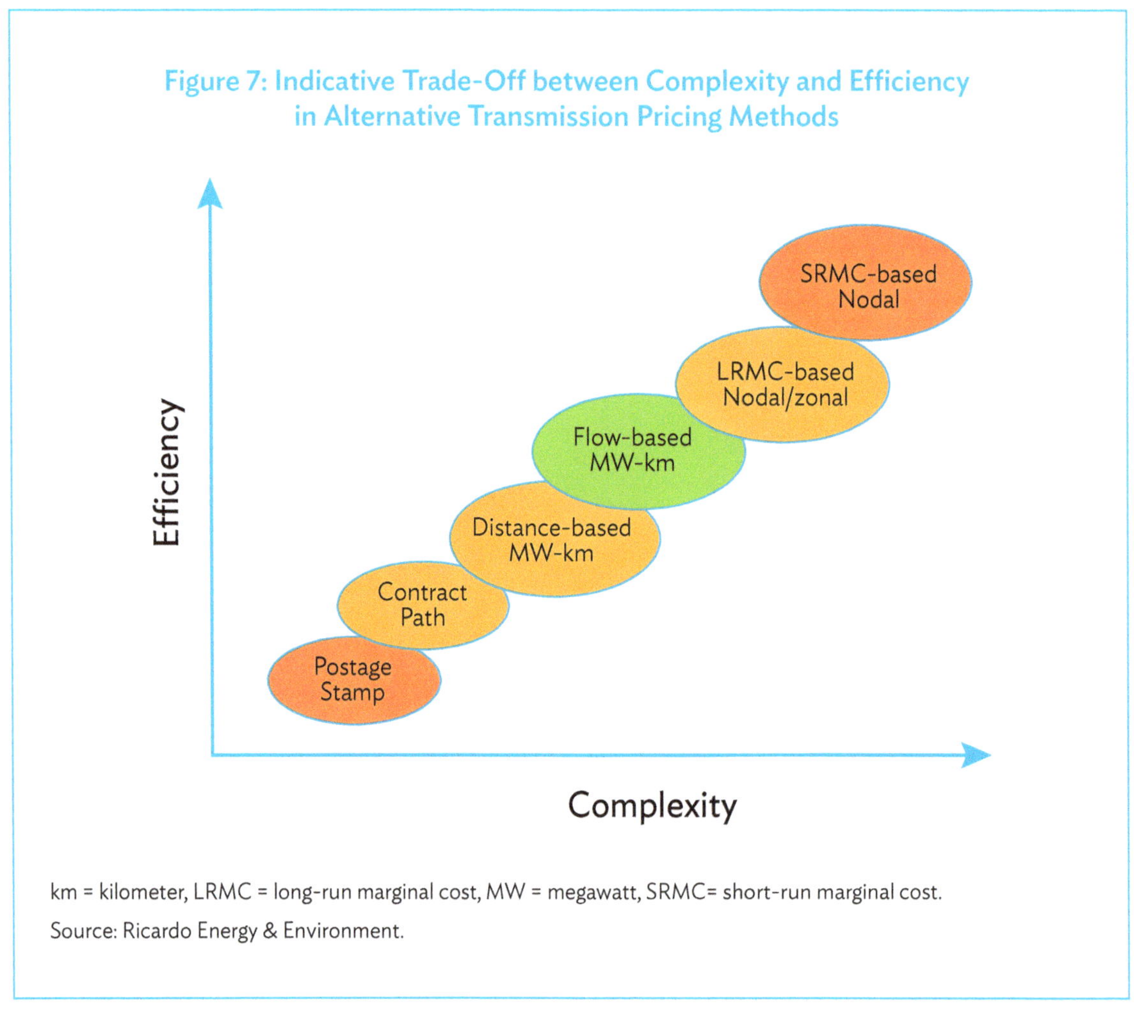

km = kilometer, LRMC = long-run marginal cost, MW = megawatt, SRMC= short-run marginal cost.

Source: Ricardo Energy & Environment.

Examples of the countries using the different approaches summarized above are given in **Table 5**. Note that in some cases, transmission charges are calculated using a combination of methods to recover different aspects of the costs. This enables provision of appropriate location signals through a portion of the transmission charges.

Table 5: Examples of International Transmission Charging Methods

Country	Postage Stamp	Contract Path	Distance-based (MW-km)	Flow-based (MW-km)	LRMC-based nodal/zonal	SRMC-based nodal
United Kingdom[a]					✓	
Ireland	✓				✓	
Australia	✓			✓		
Brazil					✓	
New Zealand	✓					
Europe (ENTSO-E)[b]	✓					
SAPP				✓		
WAPP (Proposed)				✓		

ENTSO-E = European Network of Transmission System Operators for Electricity, km= kilometer, LRMC = long-run marginal cost, MW = megawatt, SAPP = Southern African Power Pool, SRMC = short-run marginal cost, WAPP = West African Power Poo.

[a] National Grid in United Kingdom calculates charges using a flow-based transport model but with unit costs of transmission built up using expansion costs based on LRMC principles. Charges are applied on a zonal basis.

[b] In continental Europe, cross-border transmission charges are calculated from an assessment of the proportion of the energy supplied by each national network that arises from transits through the network arising from neighbouring country transfers. A compensation sum is then agreed by the ENTSO-E members, which is allocated to the countries contributing to cross-border flows in proportion to their energy imports and exports.

Sources: (Australia) Transgrid. TransGrid Pricing Methodology, 2015/16 – 2017/18. https://www.transgrid.com.au/what-we-do/our-network/our-pricing/Documents/TransGrid%27s%20Pricing%20Methodology%20%20201516%20–%20201718.pdf; (Brazil) F. Salcedo and K. Porter. 2013. *Regulatory Framework and Cost Regulations for the Brazilian National Grid (Transmission System): Final Report*. Columbia, Maryland: Exeter Associates Inc. http://www.raponline.org/wp-content/uploads/2016/05/exeter-salcedoporter-braziltransmissioncostregulationreport-2013-october.pdf; and Agência Nacional de Energia Elétrica. 2016. *Estabelecimento das Tarifas de Uso do Sistema de Trasnmissão – TUST para o ciclo 2016–2017*. Brasilia: Superintendência de Gestão Tarifária, ANEEL. http://www.consultaesic.cgu.gov.br/busca/dados/Lists/Pedido/Attachments/485318/RESPOSTA_PEDIDO_48581-001991-2016-00.pdf; (Europe) European Commission Regulation. 2010. Commission Regulation No. 838/2010 of 23 September 2010 on laying down guidelines relating to the inter-transmission system operator compensation mechanism and a common regulatory approach to transmission charging. *Official Journal of the European Union*. http://eur-lex.europa.eu/LexUriServ/LexUriServ.do?uri=OJ:L:2010:250:0005:0011:EN:PDF.; (United Kingdom) National Grid ESO. 2019. *Connection and Use of System Code*. https://www.nationalgrid.com/uk/electricity/codes/connection-and-use-system-code; (Ireland) Grid and System Operator for Northern Ireland. 2017. *Proposed 2017/2018 Generator Transmission Use of System (GTUoS) Tariffs*. 24 July. EirGrid/SONI. http://www.eirgridgroup.com/site-files/library/EirGrid/Proposed-1718-Generator-Transmission-Use-of-System-(GTUoS)-Tariffs.pdf; (New Zealand) Electricity Authority. 2019. Schedule 12.4 of the *Electricity Industry Participation Code 2010*. https://www.ea.govt.nz/code-and-compliance/the-code/part-12-transport/schedule-12-4/; (Southern African Power Pool) 2001. SAPP Transmission Wheeling Study, Phase 2 (for the Department for International Development in Southern Africa). Power Planning Associates Ltd.;

(West African Power Pool) ECOWAS Regional Electricity Regulatory Authority. Resolution No. 006/ERERA/15: Adoption of the Tariff Methodology for Regional Transmission Cost and Tariff. http://icc.ecowapp.org/sites/default/files/Transmission%20Tariff%20Methodology%20-%20August%202015-V4_signed.pdf.

5.7 Evolution of Pricing Methodologies

As experience is gained with the application of transmission charging methodologies, it is common for transmission utilities to refine the approaches used and to apply greater sophistication. In the Southern African Power Pool (SAPP), for example, a postage stamp wheeling charge was applied initially, under which charges were based on a fixed proportion of the costs of the energy wheeled. Countries making their network assets available to buyers and sellers of energy for wheeling purposes received payments calculated as a fixed percentage of the value of the energy being wheeled.

After gaining several years of operating experience, SAPP changed the method to a flow-based MW-km approach, which sought to identify the specific assets used by each physical bilateral trade and calculate charges based on the proportion of the asset's capacity that is being used for wheeling purposes. Further refinements to the methodology were then investigated to develop a method that was compatible with the introduction of a spot market for energy trading, rather than restricting energy transactions to physical bilateral trades.

Importantly, that whatever initial approach is adopted in the GMS, the possibility exists for this to be refined later and for adjustments to the methodology to be introduced based on operational experience.

5.8 Proposed Approach

The core principles that have been considered when designing a wheeling framework for GMS countries are to ensure that

- **full cost recovery is achieved on interconnection assets** with reasonable returns on equity and attractive terms for investors;
- the methodology treats all network users **fairly** and in a **nondiscriminatory** manner; and
- both the **simplicity** of implementing the methodology, and its **longevity** are observed. Investors in transmission and distribution projects need to be assured of the stability of the charges.

Figure 8 shows the fundamental steps in the proposed methodology.

Calculate the value of each regional asset, and derive the annual asset revenue requirements for the owner

- The Regional Transmission Network consists of all interconnected assets at voltage levels greater than or equal to 110 kilovolts (kV) or as otherwise agreed by the relevant regional coordination body Regional Power Trade Coordination Committee (RPTCC) or, in the future, a Regional Power Coordination Centre (RPCC) in the GMS. Interconnected assets are all those that are regionally interconnected, even if there are two or more synchronous areas. They do not include low-voltage interconnections, supplying a small domestic demand from one country to another.
- Importantly, the assets included in the wheeling asset database should take into account all the transmission equipment in the network, including transmission lines, cables, switchgear (i.e., circuit breakers, disconnectors, and protection equipment), transformers, and other ancillary equipment such as reactive compensation equipment installed on the network that is not covered by ancillary services payments.

Figure 8: Typical Wheeling Arrangement through a Regional Transmission Network

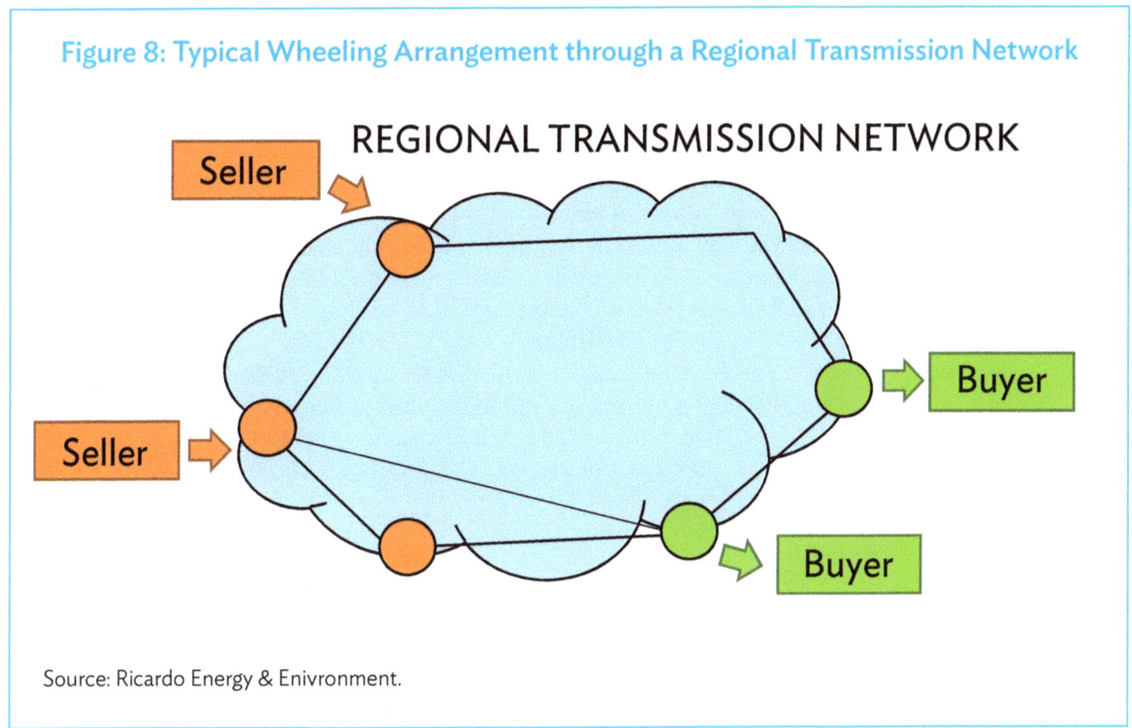

Source: Ricardo Energy & Enivronment.

- The value of the transmission assets in the GMS vertically integrated utilities might not be known for historical reasons, but the replacement value can be calculated from recent projects and can be a publicly available information. It is proposed that the regional transmission asset database be kept by the RPCC. The network assets included in the database will be updated annually from information provided by each national transmission utility. The RPCC will keep a database of the standardized costs for each of the assets in the asset database. Equipment costs should be stated as installed costs including civil works.
- A rate-of-return framework is proposed, whereby the annual revenue requirements for each asset are the sum of three components:
  (i) the annual capital allowance (covering the cost of depreciation),
  (ii) the annual return allowance (covering the cost of financing the asset), and
  (iii) the O&M allowance (covering the costs of operating and maintaining the asset), where

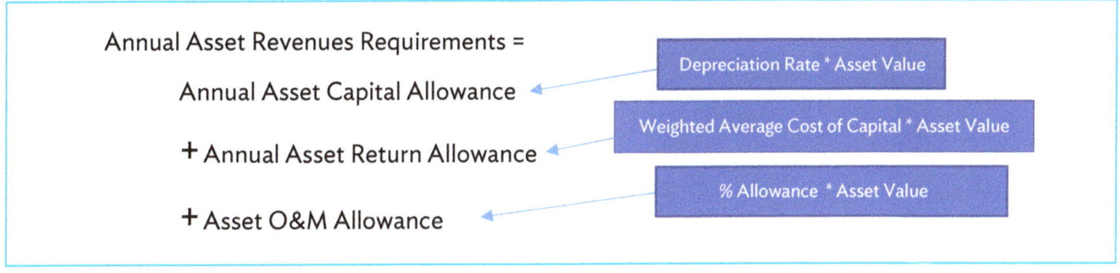

- Linear depreciation is advised, assuming that all assets within the same category (e.g., transmission lines, transformers) have the same economic life. Standard economic lives would be determined and agreed upon by the RPCC. Alternatively, for simplicity purposes, a single asset value can be chosen.
- The asset's weighted average cost of capital (WACC) reflects the true cost of financing the asset, including the return expected by equity shareholders, the interest of the debt contracted to pay for the asset, and the impact of corporate taxes when applicable.
- The WACC values allowed will be agreed by the RPCC. Ideally, all countries should use the same WACC values for regional interconnector asset value calculation. A common WACC for all countries in the GMS will depend on factors such as the differences in the risks of investing in individual countries and foreign exchange risk, and may be hard to agree in practice. While agreeing a single region-wide value would be desirable for ease of implementation, it would be possible to allow different figures to be adopted by individual countries, subject to the agreement of all GMS members represented in the RPCC. Consideration could be given to adopting a cap on the maximum value of the WACC values, again subject to agreement by the RPCC.

Derive trade revenue requirements from estimated asset utilization

For each trade, use system simulations to derive the trade revenue requirements from the estimated utilization of each regional asset by a particular trade.

- System simulations are performed by the RPCC using load flow analysis, representing the regional system at peak time for the following year.
- First a simulation including all regional trades is performed (the Base Case).
- For each trade, the Base Case is compared with a trade-specific scenario where all regional trades except the one trade that is being examined are included in the system. This particular trade is "removed" from the load flow model by decreasing the consumption by the trade volume at the transmission node associated with the demand (or at the border between countries).
- The trade is then replaced and the transmission elements on which the flow increased by more than 1% are identified and defined as the transmission assets utilized for the specific regional bilateral trade. The percentage of the rating of the asset used by the trade is defined as the "utilization rate" of the asset by this particular trade (Figures 9 and 10).
- The annual revenue requirements for each asset from this particular trade is derived from the utilization rate of this asset, and the total annual revenue requirements for this asset, where.

> *Annual Asset Revenue Requirement from a trade t =*
>
> Annual Asset Revenue Requirement x Asset Utilization Rate for trade t

- The total annual revenue requirements from the trade is the sum of the annual asset revenue requirements for all assets utilized in this trade.

Figure 9: Base Case for Analysis

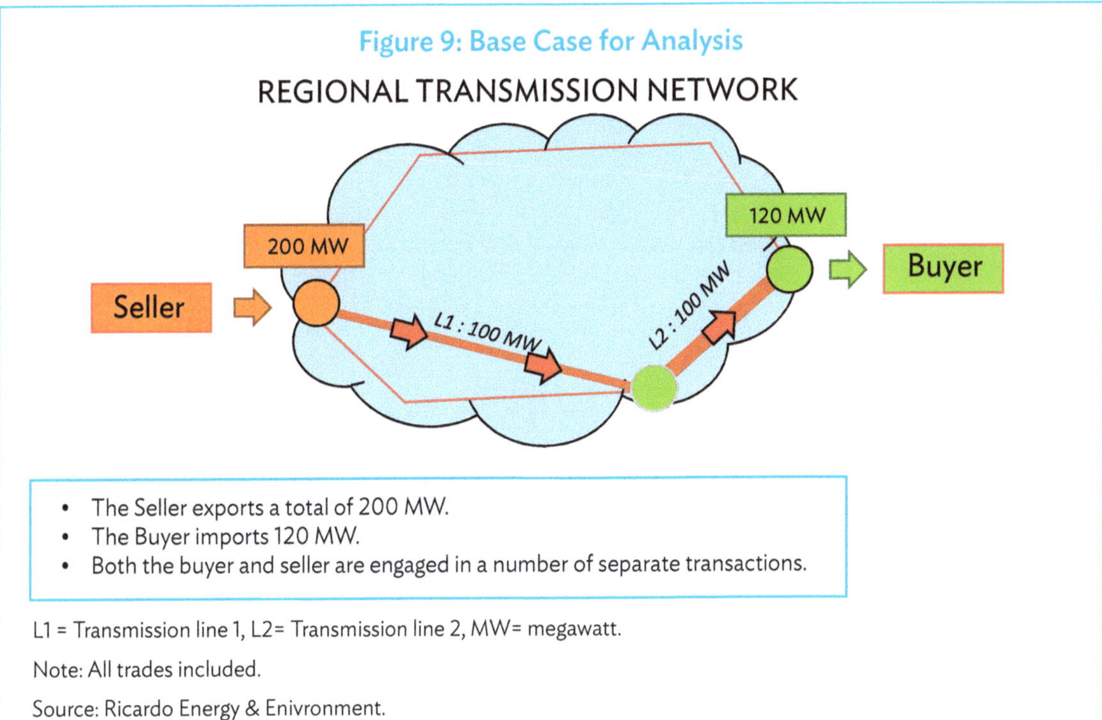

- The Seller exports a total of 200 MW.
- The Buyer imports 120 MW.
- Both the buyer and seller are engaged in a number of separate transactions.

L1 = Transmission line 1, L2= Transmission line 2, MW= megawatt.

Note: All trades included.

Source: Ricardo Energy & Enivronment.

Figure 10: Trade-Specific Scenario

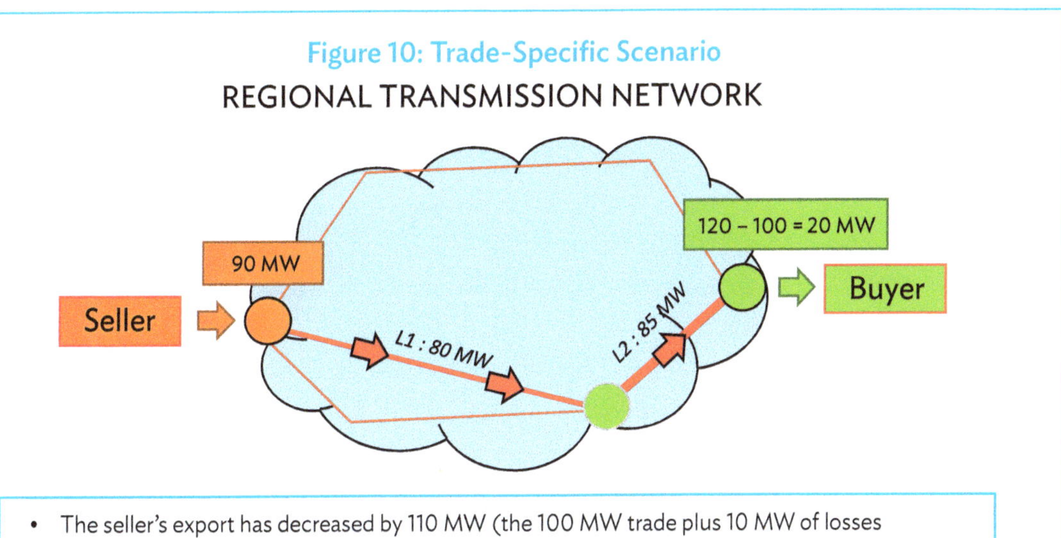

- The seller's export has decreased by 110 MW (the 100 MW trade plus 10 MW of losses associated with the trade.
- L1's utilization has decreased by 20% after removing the 100 MW trade.
- L2's utilization has decreased by 15% after removing the 100 MW trade.
- Both L1 and L2 are defined as transmission assets used by this trade.
- This trade needs to recover 2% of L1's revenue requirement and 4% of L2's revenue requirement.

L1 = Transmission line 1, L2= Transmission line 2, MW= megawatt.

Note: 100 MW trade and associated 10 MW losses removed.

Source: Ricardo Energy & Enivronment.

Use system simulations to estimate the total system losses incurred by each trade

- Similarly, to assess losses, system simulations are performed by the RPCC using load flow analysis, representing the regional system at peak time for the following year. A simulation including all regional trades is performed (the base case), and compared with trade-specific scenarios.
- The transmission losses associated with a particular trade are calculated by looking at the change in active power at the node of injection for this trade, between the base case (including all trades) and the trade-specific scenario (excluding this particular trade), where

Losses incurred by a trade t =

Active power at injection node with the trade (base case scenario)

- Trade Volume

- Active power at injection node without the trade (trade-specific scenario)

- If the value is negative, then the bilateral trade reduces transmission losses. A decision to make in implementing the methodology is whether this reduction in losses should be credited to the trading parties.
- This calculation process is shown conceptually in Figures 11 and 12.

Figure 11: Base Case

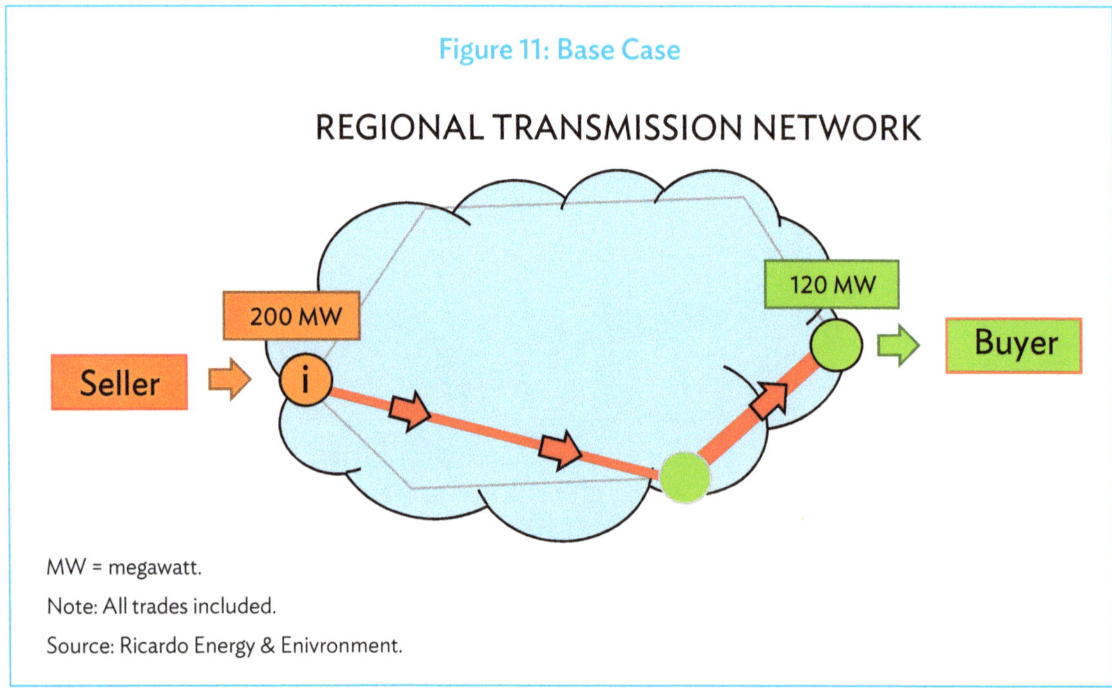

MW = megawatt.

Note: All trades included.

Source: Ricardo Energy & Enivronment.

Figure 12: Trade-Specific Scenario

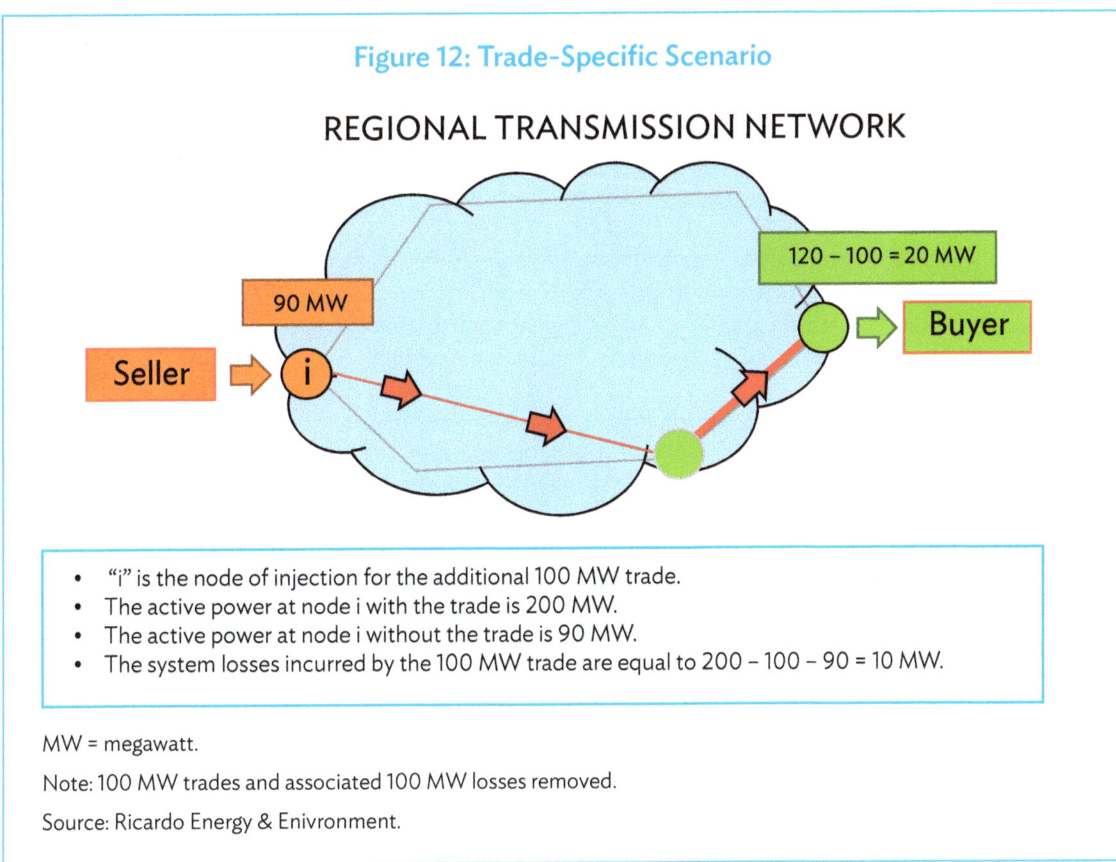

- "i" is the node of injection for the additional 100 MW trade.
- The active power at node i with the trade is 200 MW.
- The active power at node i without the trade is 90 MW.
- The system losses incurred by the 100 MW trade are equal to 200 – 100 – 90 = 10 MW.

MW = megawatt.

Note: 100 MW trades and associated 100 MW losses removed.

Source: Ricardo Energy & Enivronment.

Derive total wheeling charge

For each trade, derive the total wheeling charge from each asset's annual revenue requirement

- The total annual wheeling charge per MWh (megawatt hour) for each trade is calculated from the total annual transmission revenue requirements from the trade and the energy scheduled to be traded, where
- The transmission losses are payable by the purchaser of the regional bilateral trade. The price payable for the energy is determined by the RPCC. Alternatively, an "in-kind" settlement of the losses associated with the trade could be implemented, whereby the generation output of the seller of the regional bilateral trade is increased by the transmission losses percentage.

Total wheeling charge for a trade t (per MWh) =

$$\frac{\text{Annual Asset Revenue Requirement from trade t}}{\text{Energy Scheduled to be traded}}$$

5.9 Recommendations for Implementation

The load flow-based methodology outlined above is proposed as the most appropriate for bilateral trading and provides the most appropriate economic signals for multiple users of regional transmission networks. The method allows for full recovery of private transmission project costs and a fair and transparent allocation of usage for the utilities used for wheeling.

The determination of transmission costs and revenue requirements is best done by the RPCC using standard published costs for transmission assets for historical infrastructure and actual costs for future infrastructure. The RPCC would also be the most logical body to hold the "master" transmission system models needed to calculate wheeling charges for the GMS as a whole.

To develop the application of this methodology to regional power trades in the GMS, it is proposed that sample calculations are undertaken for sample individual interconnectors and grid-to-grid transactions. This undertaking will explore the data and models needed to perform the wheeling charge calculations and enable a more detailed examination of the practical aspects of the methodology.

The testing of the wheeling charge methodology should be undertaken in conjunction with further development of the licensing and commercial arrangements discussed earlier (see Section 4.2).

To enable wheeling at the institutional level, there needs to be a regulatory structure in place in GMS countries, that enables the body charged with taking regulatory decisions to operate at arm's length from

- any of the parties engaged in the ownership or operation of power system assets; and
- any utility or private-owned company that is trading the electricity.

5.10 Detailed Statement of Proposed Wheeling Charge Methodology

A detailed statement of the proposed methodology for calculating wheeling charges in the GMS is included in Appendix 4. Appendix 5 shows an example of the way that wheeling charges would be calculated for a bilateral trade using existing transmission assets.

6 Short-Term Bilateral Trading Measures

At present, there is no standardized approach to regional power trading in the Greater Mekong Subregion (GMS). All existing contracts have been set up on a case by case basis and are based on the negotiation of long-term bilateral contracts. The model that is most prevalent is the independent power producer (IPP) approach, with individual PPAs being negotiated and entered into between IPPs and national power utilities. Furthermore, because of the varying degrees of unbundling of the electricity sectors in GMS countries, there is no defined model for potential sellers to easily identify potential trading parties.

As the level of interconnectivity of GMS countries increases, so do the opportunities for short-term trading using spare transmission capacity. In situations where hydrological and demand patterns vary, or where power station outputs are constrained because of outages, for example, purchasing power for a period of hours to a few days ahead can be highly attractive to utilities. This tends to strengthen the need for an efficient short-term bilateral trading environment.

Creating a common trading platform would have significant benefits over the current approach, including

- giving visibility to all market participants of available offers to sell and buy power, and standardizing trading agreements. This would simplify the commercial process leading to a signed power purchase agreement (PPA) between parties;
- establishing competition among sellers. Creating a liquid short-term bilateral market would potentially lead to lower energy prices in the region;
- embedding wheeling fees and loss factors within the bilateral trading process. This would facilitate trading among all market participants (and not just those sharing a border in common or within the same network), and provide the appropriate commercial incentives for transmission owners and system operators to participate in wheeling; and
- giving a coordination and supervision role to the Regional Power Coordination Centre (RPCC) that would enable it to better support dispatch, planning, settlement, and balancing activities across the network.

In the most general case, a short-term bilateral trade (STBT) needs to be designed to allow trading of surplus energy between any pair of GMS countries, eventually using transmission facilities of a third regional country. This trade should utilize the surplus capacity of lines linked to existing PPAs or the available capacity that exists on the third country system.

STBT should ideally be possible in the time frames from year-ahead to on-the-day (one hour before real time). The proposed interim arrangements for the GMS focus on trading down to the day ahead of real time system operation.

6.1 Proposed Interim Arrangements

The highest priority for short-term trading is to enable

- surplus energy from IPPs to be sold using "spare" transmission capacity on existing interconnectors,
- seasonal surpluses in one country to be sold to another country, and
- the purchase of power when there are unforeseen shortages.

Trading should therefore be permitted down to the day before real time as a priority to maximize the benefits of these trades.

At its simplest, short-term trading requires an assessment of the available transfer capability (ATC) on the relevant interconnector(s) and/or third-party transmission system to ensure that a trade is physically feasible, and then a simple means of contracting for the energy that is to be transferred.

Initially, it would be possible to extend the use of existing bilateral contract structures from long-term multi-year contracts (the current arrangement) to short-term bilateral trades. However, the more general case of short-term trading in the GMS is considered here, exploring alternative contracting arrangements.

The proposed interim arrangements would be based on the following principles, which are broadly similar to those used in the Southern African Power Pool (SAPP), and are compatible with an evolutionary process beginning with short-term physical bilateral contracts and then adding further sophistication to the market as the trading parties' experience grows.

Submit Registration Request to the RPCC. Buyers and sellers can choose to "opt-out" from a **published list of potential buyers and sellers** produced by the RPCC on a monthly basis. If they chose to be excluded from this list, they are still allowed to trade, but their contact details and intention to trade would remain confidential.

Sellers offer short-term bilateral trades. Potential sellers can make offers of short-term bilateral trades (STBTs) for the next day/week up to one rolling year ahead. These offers, at the discretion of the seller, can be either

- *public:* the seller sends the offer to the RPCC, which distributes it to all registered buyers; or
- *restricted:* the seller only sends the offer with one or several potential buyers, at its own discretion, either by fax, e-mail, or using a dedicated webpage. Some market participants may see this as a transitional option between current and proposed "public distribution" arrangements.

Buyers check trade feasibility. Interested buyers consult the latest Available Transfer Capability (ATC) report and evaluate the technical feasibility of trade.

- ATC reports are circulated by the RPCC every week for the rolling year ahead to each potential buyer. Updates are shared with all potential buyers every time a new trade is approved by the RPCC.
- ATC reports will enable interested buyers to confirm that sufficient technical capacity exists to accommodate both the long-term bilateral contract capacity that has been reserved on the relevant interconnector and the proposed short-term trade.
- ATC is typically defined with reference to the total transfer capability (TTC) on an interconnection and the need for a transmission reliability margin (TRM) on the interconnector, to cater for contingency situations.

  Thus,

  $$ATC = TTC - TRM$$

- Factors to be included in the TRM allowance should include both additional power flows that may result to transmission circuit outages, and the possible need for reserve power to flow between one network and another in the event of a generation shortfall.
- An automated algorithm could be developed to enable this calculation, and there would be a need for the system operators to work collaboratively or for the RPCC to calculate and publish the predicted ATC figures at different time scales.

Buyers evaluate selling offers. Interested buyers consult the latest Transmission Charges and Loss Factors reports and evaluate the "value for money" of the selling offer.

- A Transmission Charges and Transmission Loss Factors Report is published by the RPCC at the start of each trading year.
- The combination of loss factor and transmission charges reports will allow interested buyers to estimate the trade volume net of network losses (i.e., the net power/energy delivered to them) and the total price (including wheeling and energy fees) payable for a given trade.
- Ideally, transmission charges and loss factors will have been calculated according to the methodology highlighted in Chapter 5.
- Alternatively, for an interim period, these values could be calculated as a simple percentage of the value of the relevant trade allocated to each country providing a wheeling service.

Pro-form draft contract signed. Interested buyers can sign a pro-forma draft contract with the seller.

- This should indicate as a minimum the identity of the buyer and the seller, the trade volume in MW, the schedule, and the agreed price.
- Other standard legal conditions should be developed and then embedded in the pro-forma contract.

Draft contract sent to RPCC. The draft contract between seller and buyer is sent by the buyer to the RPCC for final acceptance.

- Acceptance by the RPCC is solely based on the criteria of technical feasibility (based on the ATC table reflecting all trades accepted to date). It is not proposed that the RPCC make decisions whether a given trade is commercially or economically viable.

- Requests for acceptance are made by email only to the RPCC, and are treated in a first-come-first-served basis.
- The delivery receipt generated by the seller's computer can be used as evidence of the time of acceptance of the trade.

Inform buyer and seller of agreed trade volume. Upon acceptance by the RPCC, the wheelers, buyer, and seller are informed of the agreed trade volume

- Buyer and seller are notified by the RPCC of the acceptance within one working day.
- The ATC table is updated accordingly.

Buyer, seller, and wheeler/s sign a contract.

Define settlement process. A simple settlement process involving the buyer, wheeler, and seller directly would be defined, ideally in the PPA.

- The seller invoices buyer for contracted energy. Energy that is inadvertently not provided or over-provided is not part of the invoicing.
- Wheeler/s invoice(s) buyer for wheeling revenue, and account is settled by the buyer.

6.2 Proposed Long-Term Arrangements

- In the future, market participants could be given an opportunity—through short-term bilateral trading—to re-trade their physical position into balance up to one hour ahead. Market participants would enter offers of energy for sale on a bulletin board, which is essentially an automated web-based tool offering visibility of the potential trades that could be entered across the region.
- Market participants would view all valid offers on the bulletin board, which are inclusive of transmission charges and losses, and takes account of ATC. Each buyer thus sees the net price and MW of all possible transactions with them. A buyer can accept a part, or all of the transaction. A seller can change their offer at any time. When a transaction is accepted by the buyer, it is binding on both parties. Nonetheless, a buyer and a seller can re-trade their position at any time before market closure.
- In the future, potential buyers would be able to propose bids to purchase energy in the same way sellers can make offers. This second phase would allow sellers to change their offers to meet a bid and hope that the buyer will accept.
- Each offer would have a start and end date, a start-up time, minimum off-take energy power, and minimum/maximum off-take energy. The energy can be offered as being available the whole day, only in peak hours, or only in off-peak hours. Essentially there can be an offer for each power plant with spare capacity.
- Each offer will contain sufficient information for the RPCC to perform settlements. This way, the settlement process will be harmonized and the risk of errors will be reduced.
- This process is summarized in Figure 13.

Figure 13: Summary of the Proposed Short-Term Bilateral Trading Process

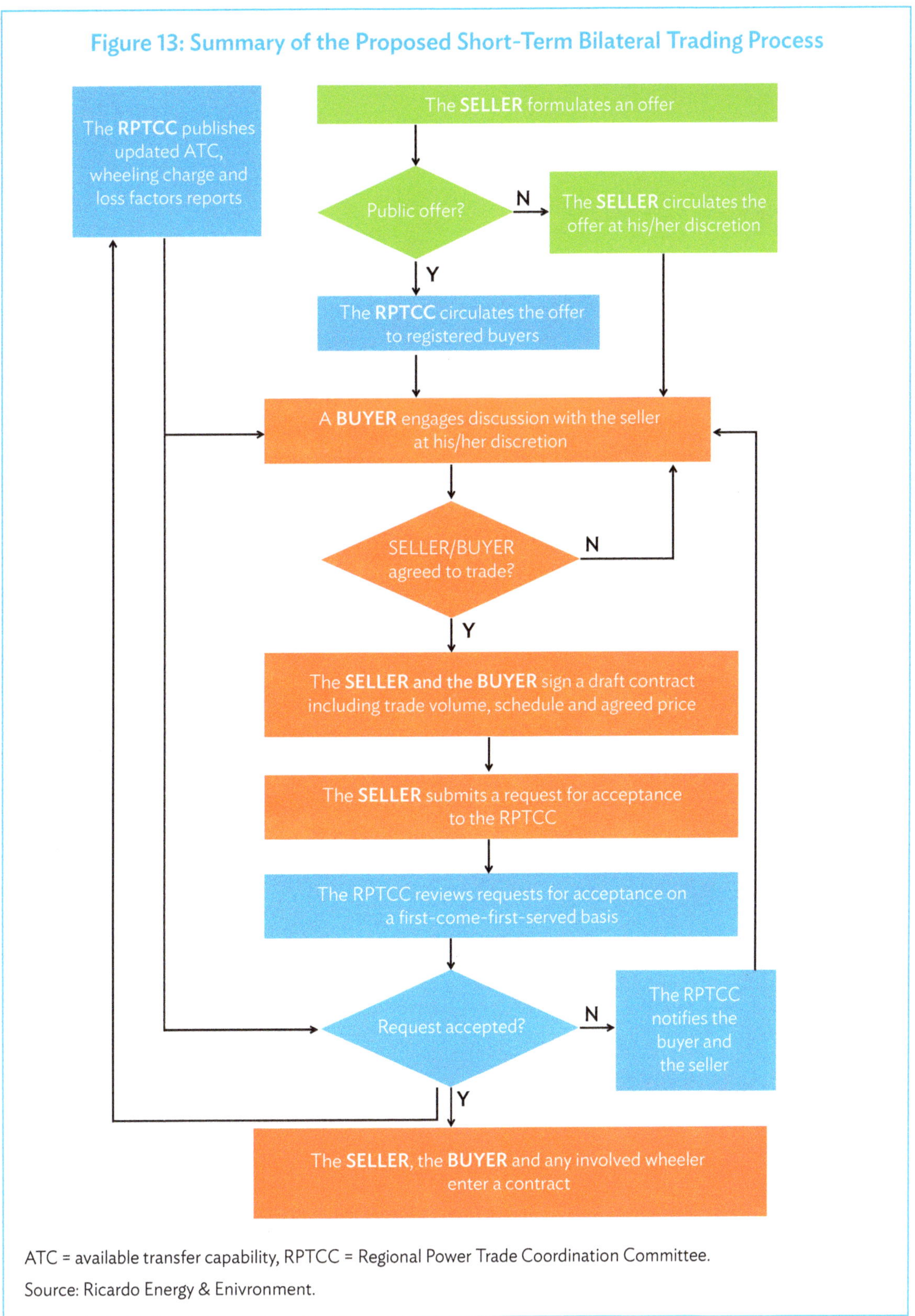

ATC = available transfer capability, RPTCC = Regional Power Trade Coordination Committee.

Source: Ricardo Energy & Enivronment.

6.3 Role of the Regional Power Coordination Centre

It is clear from the description of the short-term bilateral trading process (see Section 6.1) that the RPCC has a central role to play in several key areas, including

- assessing ATC;
- publishing ATC reports;
- circulating offers of energy for purchase by potential buyers;
- reviewing proposed trades for technical acceptability; and
- performing settlement on behalf of buyers and sellers, and playing the role of a market operator, should the short-term electricity market evolve in the future.

In addition, the proposed methodology for wheeling charges defines roles and responsibilities for the RPCC regarding the execution of power system studies and cost analysis, and determines the wheeling charges that should be applicable to any regional trade.

This list of responsibilities would represent a significant evolution from the current position, in which the RPTCC acts as a coordinating body with a largely advisory role to the stakeholders it represents in GMS member countries. There is, however, a key role for a regional market operator or Regional Power Coordination Centre (RPCC) in facilitating the processes needed to support regional power trade.

This study, therefore, recognizes the need to define the role of a RPCC and the institutional arrangements that would support the introduction of such a body. The RPCC should then be staffed continually by qualified technical, financial, and administrative personnel.

7 Balancing Mechanism

When a power trade is scheduled to take place, there are many reasons why actual power flows may differ from those agreed and scheduled between parties. For example,

- the seller may retain some of the power contracted due to a deficit of supply in its own system;
- the buyer's network may be too constrained to absorb the power scheduled in full; or
- the wheeler may not have the capability to transfer all the power scheduled from the seller to the buyer.

Any failure of parties to meet their obligations to produce or consume energy when engaging in international trade can result in imbalances on the power system. Reconciling the differences that arise between scheduled energy transfers and actual exchanges is necessary to compensate utilities if they provide energy to maintain the equilibrium of the power system.

At present, there is no standardized approach in the Greater Mekong Subregion (GMS) to settling imbalances between neighbouring networks. Specific settlement conditions are typically set out in power purchase agreements (PPAs), and these normally take the form of "in-kind" settlements, under which energy shortfalls are made good at times and in quantities agreed between the parties on an ad hoc basis.

A harmonized balancing methodology across the region would have significant benefits over the current approach, such as

- knowing imbalance calculation and settlement arrangements ahead of entering a contract will reassure to existing and potential market participants and facilitate regional power trading;
- incentivizing the in-kind settlement of imbalances during periods corresponding to when they occurred in the first place (e.g., time of day, season) will improve the fairness and non discriminatory nature of regional trading; and
- enabling cash settlement of imbalances after in-kind settlement attempts have failed will ensure that all imbalances are settled within an acceptable time frame.

7.1 Recommendations for the Identification and Reporting of Imbalances

Inadvertent Energy is defined as the difference between the net **scheduled** energy on the regional transmission assets in a national system operator's network and the net actual energy **delivered** on the assets in that network, where

Inadvertent Energy (MWh) =

Actual Net Interchange (MWh) - Scheduled Net Interchange (MWh)

Below are recommendations

- The net scheduled energy shall include reserve trading and pseudo tie-lines (to account for any power plants with shared ownership and/or dispatch responsibilities between neighbouring national system operators).
- Each national system operator shall, through daily schedule verification and the use of reliable metering equipment, accurately account for Inadvertent Energy interchanges.
- Recognizing generation and load patterns, each national system operator shall do its best to minimize inadvertent interchange energy accumulation.
- Energy meters, with readings provided hourly to the relevant Control Centres, shall measure the power transfers at each Point of Interconnection between two networks.
- Inadvertent Energy interchange shall be calculated and recorded hourly and may be accumulated as a credit or debit to a national system operator or trading party (e.g., a generator or industrial consumer).

7.2 Recommendations for the "In-Kind" Settlement of Imbalances

- It is proposed that Inadvertent Energy accumulations shall be settled "in-kind" by default under interim arrangements until such time that a cash-based system has been fully implemented.
- Inadvertent Energy interchange accumulated shall be paid back during the same time-of-use and same season-of-use when it was accrued (e.g., peak, standard and/or off-peak, wet season or dry season).
- The time-of-use and season-of-use definition shall be published by the RPCC.

A possible definition of time-of-use and season-of-use periods is shown in Figure 14 (based on the definitions used by Eskom in South Africa).

The suggested arrangements for the recording, calculation, and settlement of imbalances are shown in Figure 15.

The proposed process is described in the following sections.

Figure 14: Typical Definition of Time-of-Use Periods

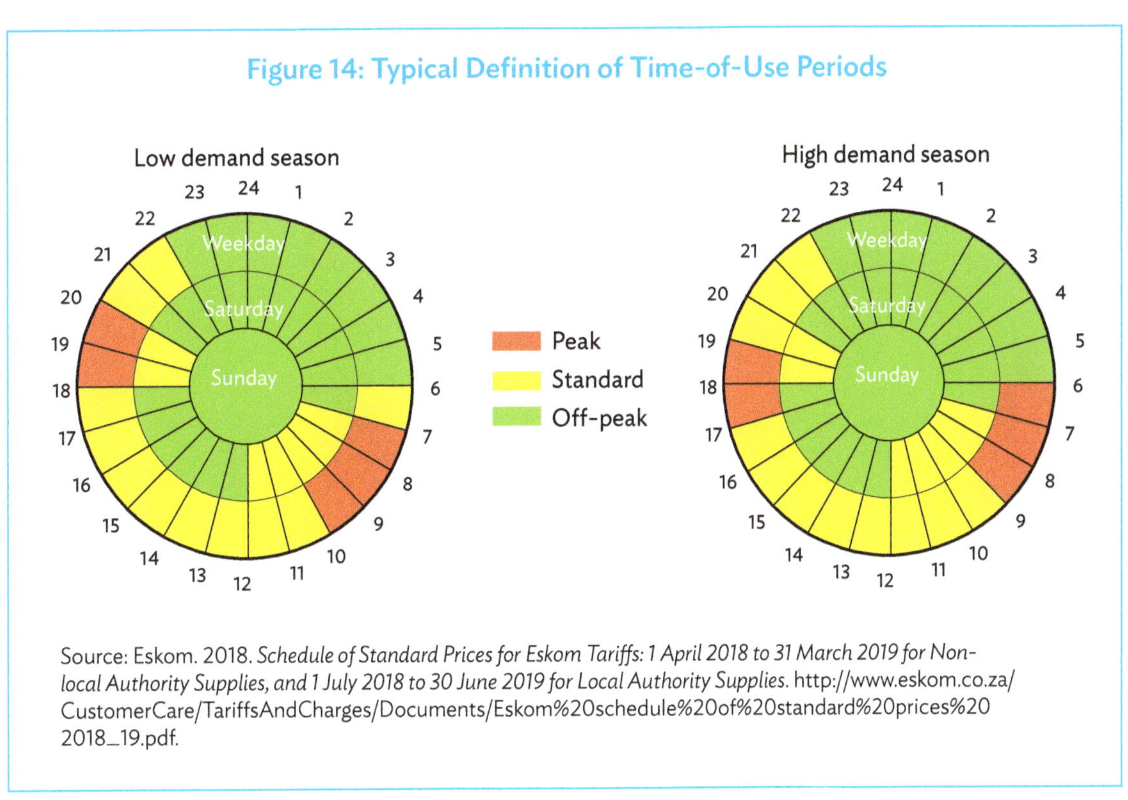

Source: Eskom. 2018. *Schedule of Standard Prices for Eskom Tariffs: 1 April 2018 to 31 March 2019 for Non-local Authority Supplies, and 1 July 2018 to 30 June 2019 for Local Authority Supplies.* http://www.eskom.co.za/CustomerCare/TariffsAndCharges/Documents/Eskom%20schedule%20of%20standard%20prices%20 2018_19.pdf.

Figure 15: Indicative Imbalance Reconciliation Timeline

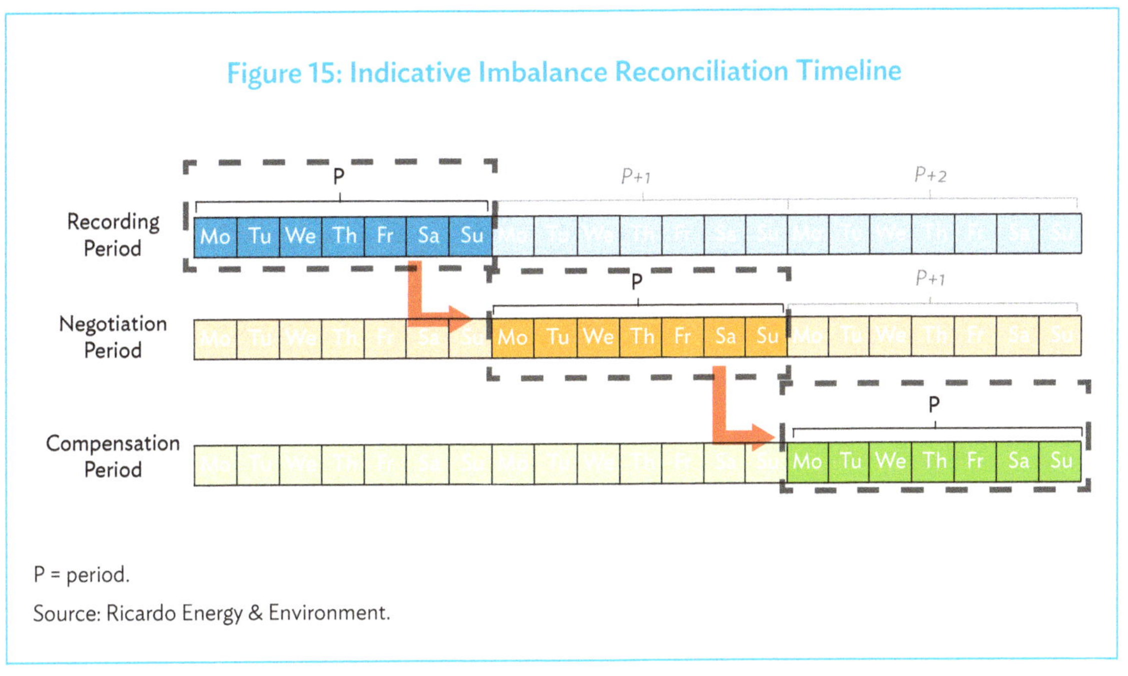

P = period.

Source: Ricardo Energy & Environment.

Weekly Inadvertent Energy submitted to RPCC. Each operator submits a weekly summary of Inadvertent Energy interchange to the RPCC over the recording period. This should be submitted by 12:00 noon on the first working day of the week.

Inadvertent Energy reconciliation. RPCC shall reconcile the Inadvertent Energy interchanges such that the sum of all interchanges is zero. The process of netting to zero shall be agreed to net off meter errors.

Offers of "in-kind" compensation. Over the following week (the negotiation period), participants who caused imbalances make offers of "in-kind" compensation. Each participant which had a shortfall shall propose a suitable time to return the Inadvertent Energy to the affected market participant(s) for the following week.

Buyer requests offer acceptance. Before the end of the negotiation period and upon reaching an agreement with the seller, the buyer requests acceptance of the proposed "in-kind" settlement by the RPCC.

If there has not been any agreement reached over the negotiation period, or if the RPCC has not been notified in due time, the imbalance shall be settled in cash.

RPCC advises acceptability of "in-kind" settlement. After checking whether there is sufficient transfer capacity to carry out the proposed "in-kind" settlement, the RPCC notifies participants, and updates and circulates the ATC reports.

Should there not be a sufficient ATC on the interconnected transmission system to enable the proposed in-kind settlement, the seller (i.e., the trading party responsible for the imbalance) shall agree on a suitable time to discuss with RPCC by the end of the negotiation period.

If there has not been any alternative agreement reached over the negotiation period, or if the RPCC has not been notified in due time, the imbalance shall be settled in cash.

7.3 Recommendations for the Cash Settlement of Imbalances

It is common to use a market's clearing price as the reference price to settle imbalances in cash. However, the GMS does not have bids and offers from balancing participants or a day-ahead market clearing price to reference.

Below are recommendations

- The proposed alternative is to have a reference price based on the definition of the marginal generating unit type on the system. The reference price is the typical price for the unit type, whether this be hydro, combined cycle gas, coal-fired generation, or open cycle gas turbine.
- A further premium could be added to the reference price, using calculation methodologies similar to those implemented in South Africa and India. Typically, this premium would be derived from system frequency at the time the imbalance occurred. The premium would penalize market participants that caused an energy shortfall due to a shortfall of generation in their own system.

The following arrangements are proposed for calculating the reference price and settling imbalances in cash.

System operators advise RPCC of generation mix. One month before the start of the trading year, each system operator shall provide the RPCC with relevant information on their generation mix. This includes the installed generation, size and type for each generating unit, the planned maintenance schedule, and the estimated unplanned maintenance percentage for the current trading year.

RPCC calculates marginal unit stack. The RPCC calculates the marginal unit stack and distributes the results to all market participants. The marginal unit is determined by adding the peak demand, the operating reserves, the planned maintenance, and unplanned maintenance (both of which could be estimated using typical ratios over total supply available or based on actual planned/unplanned maintenance in previous years). The marginal unit stack is shown graphically in Figure 16.

Figure 16: Marginal Unit Stack Formation

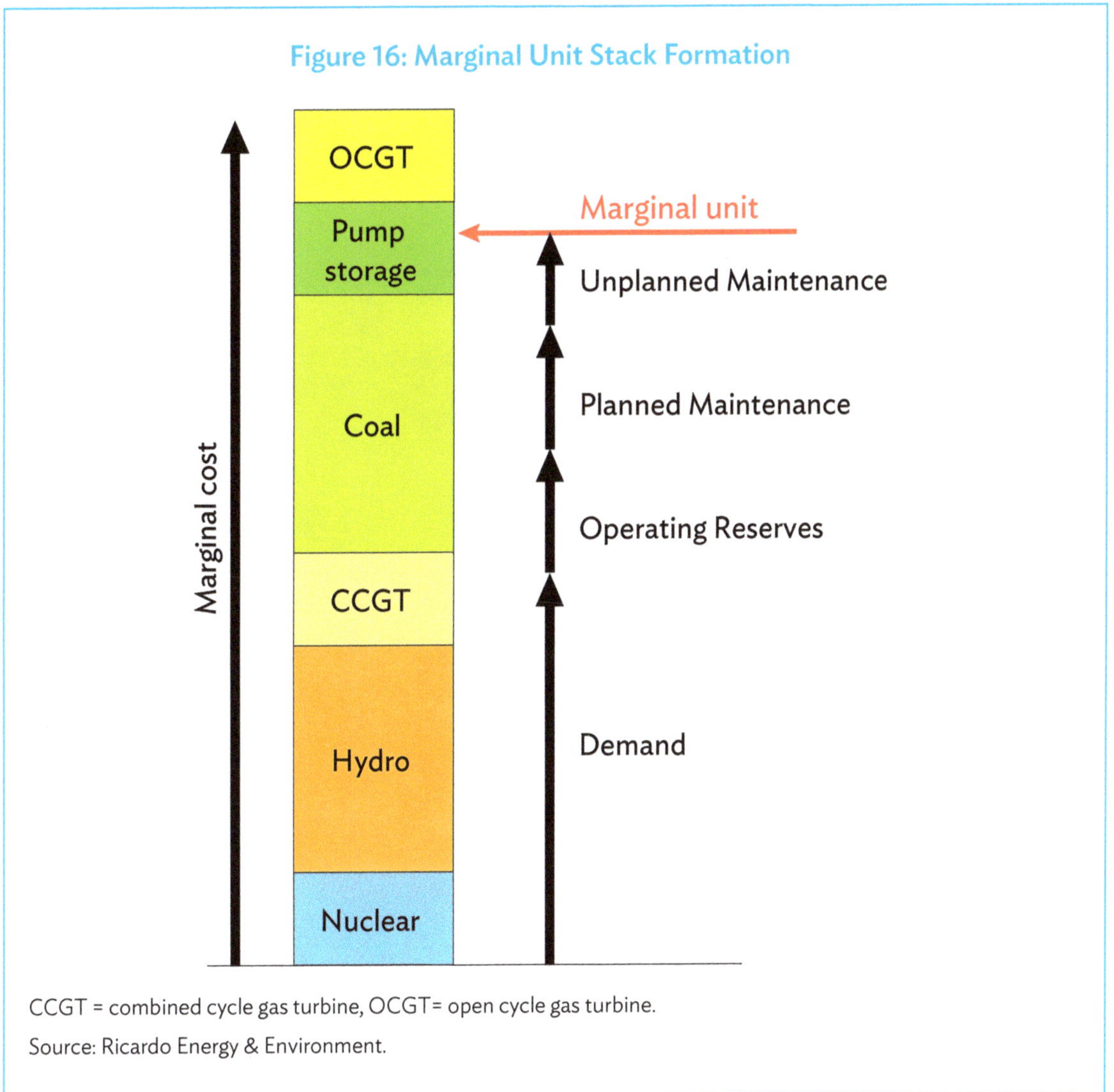

CCGT = combined cycle gas turbine, OCGT= open cycle gas turbine.

Source: Ricardo Energy & Environment.

RPCC updates merit order stack. The RPCC updates the stack monthly based on current information (e.g., fuel costs, updated planned maintenance schedules).

RPCC publishes merit order stack. The RPCC publishes the following month's balancing stack and prices to participants three working days before the first day of the next month.

Cash settlement. Invoices due to be settled in cash are derived from the monthly balancing stack. The RPCC would calculate the applicable reference price(s) (one reference price per hour) within a month of recording the imbalance, and circulate this price among the relevant parties.

7.4 Summary of Interim Arrangements

Figure 17: Summary of Interim Arrangements for Imbalance Settlement

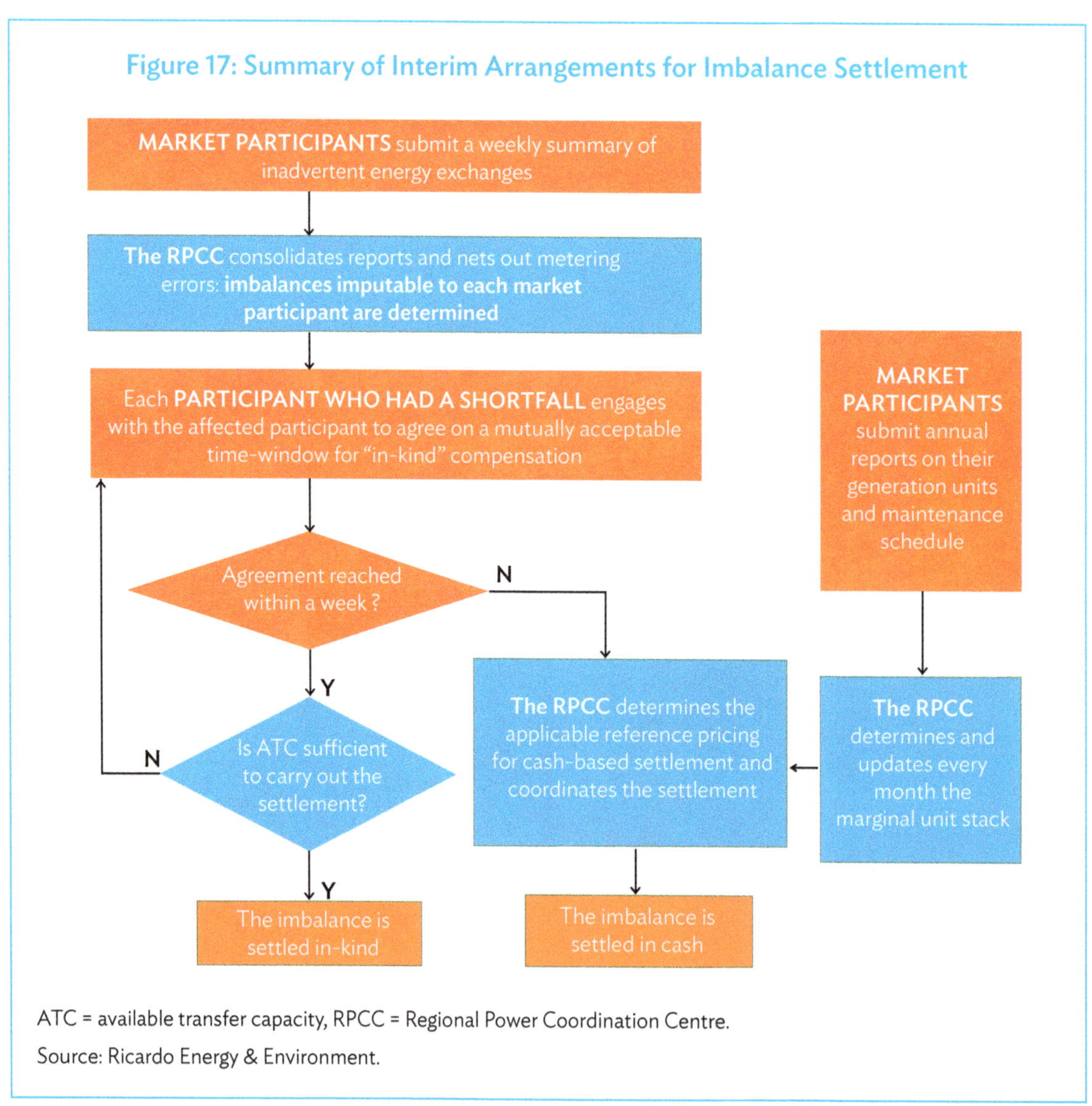

ATC = available transfer capacity, RPCC = Regional Power Coordination Centre.

Source: Ricardo Energy & Environment.

7.5 Role of the Regional Power Coordination Centre

The RPCC has a central role in the collection of data related to inadvertent energy exchanges and the validation of the meter data to ensure that the correct readings are being processed (Figure 17).

It is also responsible for assessing whether the ATC is sufficient to enable the "in-kind" settlement of imbalances, and for defining the regional unit stack that would be used for cash settlements.

These roles and responsibilities would extend beyond the remit of the current RPTCC, beyond its role as a consultative and advisory body representing GMS electricity sector stakeholders. They require the evolution of the RPTCC into a body with technical and commercial skills to act as a market operator, and with the financial standing to carry out cash settlement processes as part of the reconciliation of imbalances.

A key recommendation of this work is therefore that a regional market operator or a RPCC is created and equipped with technical and commercial skills, software, and other tools to fulfill its functions. It would be appropriate to distinguish between the roles of TSOs, which would reside with the power utilities in individual GMS countries, and the responsibilities for power trading, metering, ATC calculation, and regional transmission planning, which could be undertaken by a new regional organization. The RPCC would need the capacity and legal/commercial authority to handle financial settlements and undertake advisory functions.

8 Conclusions and Recommendations

8.1 Conclusions

Regional power trading in the Greater Mekong Subregion (GMS) has been identified by member countries as a priority area of development since the signing of the Inter-governmental Agreement on Regional Power Trade in 2002 and the associated first memorandum of understanding (MoU) in 2005.

Since then, the development of regional power trading has been limited, and has focused on the construction of dedicated transmission lines interconnecting independent power producers (IPPs) from one country to another. The ADB project Facilitating Regional Power Trading and Environmentally Sustainable Development of Electricity Infrastructure in the GMS (RETA 6440) presented a series of technical, system operations, and market design recommendations that provided a framework for the future development of regional power trade (footnote 2). Currently, regional power trading represents less than 2% of the electricity consumption in the GMS.

This raises a key question: What are the barriers preventing a greater uptake of regional power trading?

The research that has been undertaken to answer this question has highlighted a number of areas in which developments are needed to increase regional power trade. They include

- promoting an integrated approach to regional power sector planning to prepare long-term development plans collaboratively and promote the increased development of regional power transfers. This should result in improvements to system reliability, reductions in reserve margin requirements, and the potential to optimize generation resources. These benefits need to be fully understood at a regional level if the drive for interconnection and power trading is to increase;
- developing alternatives to long-term power purchase agreements (PPAs) to enable more opportunistic trading to be undertaken in the region;
- improving access to power networks for power purchase agreements (PPAs) to trade internationally, and for country to country trading through the transmission networks of third parties;
- developing equitable wheeling charges that will help ensure that the costs incurred by utilities making their network assets available to other parties for international power trading are fairly compensated;
- considering a range of regulatory arrangements and industry structures, to recognize international experience and ensure that significant institutional hurdles are not put in the way of increased trading;

- ensuring that inadvertent energy flows arising from imbalances between supply and demand caused by the non-delivery of regional trades are efficiently identified and accounted for; and
- promoting increased capacity building among GMS power utilities to ensure that staff have access to a wide range of international power sector participants and market operators and can gain confidence in how international power trading works in practice.

8.2 Lessons from Other Regional Markets and Projects

Lessons from the Southern African Power Pool

Market evolution

The evolution of the Southern Africa Power Pool (SAPP) market has taken place through a series of separate steps, with increasing sophistication.

- The market began with a simple structure of **long-term bilateral contracts**.
- These were supported by a variant of **postage-stamp wheeling charges**.
- The market was extended to include a **short-term market based** on a bulletin board, offering day-ahead trading options. **A balancing mechanism** was introduced at the same time to facilitate financial settlement of imbalances.
- A more sophisticated **day-ahead** trading platform was then introduced, based on sophisticated market clearing and zonal prices, signalling congestion in the transmission system.
- Additional **month-ahead, week-ahead, and intra-day** platforms have recently been added to increase the flexibility and options available to market participants.

This evolutionary approach, implemented over a period of some 20 years, has enabled market participants to grow in their confidence and understanding of the market.

Structure and organization

The structure and organization of the SAPP market has relied on several key high-level agreements, including

- An **Inter-Government MoU**, laying down the high-level principles of international cooperation in electricity sector planning and energy trading;
- An **Inter-Utility Memorandum of Understanding**, governing the operational arrangements between the power utilities themselves;
- An **Agreement between Operating Members**, governing the rights and responsibilities of the members and the regional organization, including the SAPP Executive Committee, Management Committee, and Coordination Centre;
- The **SAPP Operating Guidelines**, covering many of the technical areas of cooperation that would otherwise be covered by a regional Grid Code.

The existing GMS MoU-1 and MoU-2 documents lay down some of the high-level provisions that the countries have agreed to comply with regarding market development. It is recommended that a similar set of documents to those in items ii through iv above from the SAPP market are developed within the GMS, to implement a set of practical measures that will assist the development of inter-utility cooperation and regional trading.

A further recommendation relates to the establishment of the Regional Power Coordination Centre (RPCC) in the GMS as a regional coordinating body, fulfilling a similar role to the SAPP Coordination Centre.

Status of power market reforms in SAPP member countries

In Southern Africa, there are no prerequisites regarding the structure of the electricity industry in the member countries of SAPP. In each country, organizations that wish to trade are free to do so, subject to fulfilling the membership requirements of SAPP. Trading parties may include:

- vertically integrated utilities,
- single buyer organizations,
- national market operators,
- system operators,
- trader/aggregator bodies,
- wholesale buyers, or
- independent power producer.

Parties wishing to trade electricity are required to obtain permission to trade from the national regulator and apply for membership to in SAPP. In Southern Africa, there are examples of different bodies participating in the regional market, including

- South Africa (vertically integrated with international electricity trading department)
- Namibia/Zambia (single buyers)
- Botswana/Zimbabwe (system and market operators)
- Copperbelt Energy Corporation (wholesale buyer)
- Three hydro IPPs are trading in different countries
- SAPP has in principle approved an entity to be an independent trader/aggregator for multiple IPPs in multiple countries in the region.

The example of SAPP therefore reinforces the conclusion from this study: national industry structures do not need to act as a constraint to utility companies participating in a regional market.

Recommendations for establishing the Regional Power Coordination Centre as a regional body

In the RETA 6440 project, the consultants recommended that a permanent secretariat be established to follow up and monitor regional activities (footnote 2). The project also developed the concept of an RPCC. This would in many ways mirror the role of the SAPP Coordination Centre.

The key interim measures that could be envisaged prior to setting up a Coordination Centre include:

Empowering the RPTCC working groups. It is clear that the Working Group on Regulatory Issues (WGRI) and the Working Group on Performance Standards and Grid Codes (WGPG) are populated with representatives of national institutions with have strong skills and extensive experience in GMS power systems and the associated regulatory processes. From discussions with WGRI members, however, it is clear that meetings are infrequent and decision making has been limited. If these working groups were to meet more frequently, with an agenda of items delegated to them by the RPTCC, it is possible that more progress would be made in addressing issues that are technical or regulatory in nature.

Reallocating RPCC responsibilities to other bodies. The RPCC is essentially envisaged as an executing agency on behalf of the RPTCC responsible for supporting the implementation of practical measures contained in MoU-1 and MoU-2, which have shaped the structure of the GMS regional market. It is recommended that these functions be undertaken by the RPTCC itself the WGRI, and WGPG for an interim period until the RPCC has been established.

RPTCC, WGRI, and WGPG could focus their activities in key areas that would bridge the gap between short- and longer-term operations under the broad remit as a regional body of exercising advisory powers working to promote cross-border trade, and building cooperation among the national regulators and ministers on key trading issues. Other working groups should be formed, as recommended below. Specific areas of work may include the following:

- The RPTCC could play an important **promotional role** in the development of efficient electricity markets in the GMS and ensuring market transparency, while promoting non-discriminatory access to international interconnectors. This may include creating a **Working Group on Capacity Building (WGCB)** that would work with GMS utilities and regulators to identify the capacity building requirements in the region concerning international trading.
- The RPTCC may begin to provide an important platform for **information exchange between single buyers and regulators**. This would draw on the work of the **WGPG** and **WGRI** to promote and ensure development of common policies in the region. This could be achieved, for example, by the early release of a set of framework guidelines and transmission network codes that could be used by national transmission system operators (TSOs), or equivalent for capacity allocation, connection management, and balancing of transmission networks.
- The RPTCC should take responsibility for producing medium- to long-term **statements of opportunity** that show the technical and economic benefits of regional electricity trading and the opportunities that exist for new entrants into the GMS electricity sector to participate in electricity trading and boost regional development. This activity should be shared between the WGPG and the WGRI.
- The WGRI may begin its work of **advising the policy makers** in each of the member countries and sharing their views with the national regulators (or equivalent bodies) on particular issues. The committee may start to provide nonbinding opinions and recommendations in areas such as unbundling power utilities, transmission network development plans, and other grid expansion plans.
- The WGRI plays a valuable role in **developing and approving wheeling charge principles** that could be implemented to enable the two phases of power trading envisaged by Stage 2 of the GMS market opening:
  (i) trading of electricity using spare capacity that exists on transmission lines constructed across borders, and that are specifically associated with PPAs of existing power plants; and
  (ii) trading between any pair of GMS countries (if necessary, wheeling power through the transmission assets of a third country).
- **The WGPG** should work on the development and publication of a **standard grid code** for the GMS, and advise on **contractual structures and technical standards** to permit IPPs to connect to the transmission and distribution networks.
- **The RPTCC** may develop its **investigation and dispute resolution role** via a **Working Group on Market Monitoring (WGMM)**. This would monitor the electricity market and review PPAs or any inter-company transactions that are entered into by the electricity companies. The RPTCC may also act as an advisor on decisions or disputes referred to by the national

bodies. The single buyers of electricity in the member countries, national regulatory bodies, or the national TSOs (or equivalent) could refer particular issues to the RPTCC for opinions; the RPTCC may then provide advice and opinions to assist in the process of reconciling disputes. To avoid doubts, disputes to be taken up should only relate to matters involving international electricity trading; and the RPTCC may only pass judgements on the application of trading rules and contracts directly connected with cross-border trading.

In the event that disputes arise between single buyers from different territories, for example, as a result of increased interconnections between member states, it would be reasonable to assume that national regulators (or an equivalent body in the country) are made aware by the regulated utilities in each jurisdiction that the dispute has arisen; either the national regulators or the single buyers in dispute should then have the right to refer the case to the RPTCC for an opinion. The RPTCC WGMM should then review such disputes and provide an opinion to the national regulators and the single buyers (Figure 18).

Figure 18: National Regulators Refer an International Dispute to RPTCC

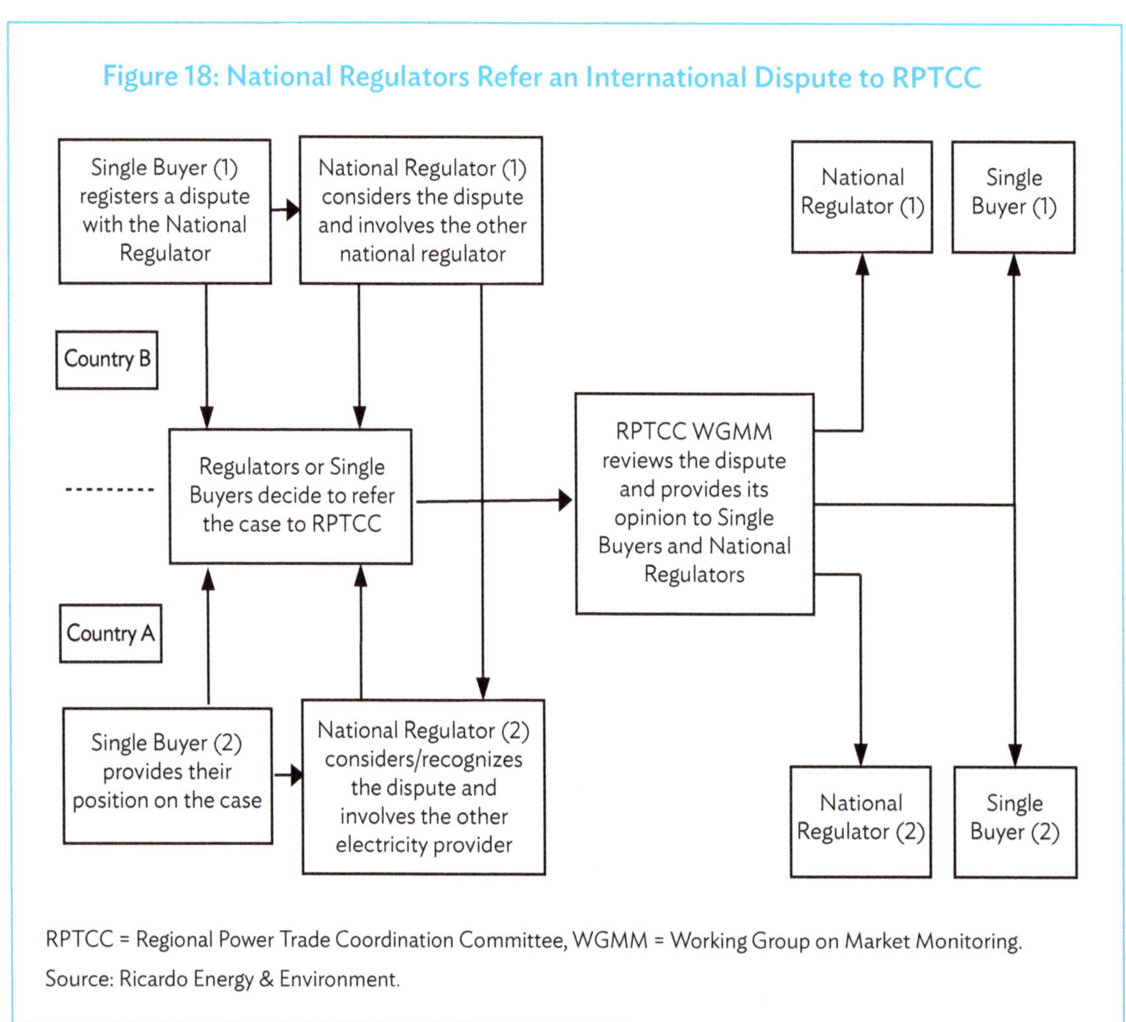

RPTCC = Regional Power Trade Coordination Committee, WGMM = Working Group on Market Monitoring.

Source: Ricardo Energy & Environment.

Lessons from the West African Power Pool

The West African Power Pool (WAPP) is at an earlier stage of development than SAPP, and it faces similar challenges in terms of seeking first to build up the level of physical interconnection between the national power systems to make regional trade more technically feasible.

WAPP has moved forward with the creation of the organizational structures and agreements necessary to permit effective interaction between the Economic Community of West African States (ECOWAS) member states in developing the market. The existence of a clearly defined set of Articles of Agreement and Regional Market Rules has paved the way for the implementation of increased trade as greater interconnectivity becomes available.

The organizational structure of WAPP, like SAPP, takes a hierarchical approach in which operational aspects of the market are devolved to a series of committees operating at the level beneath the Executive Board. Above the Board is the General Assembly, a body that has the highestlevel representation from 29 WAPP member utilities. Beneath the Executive Board is the Secretariat, whose function includes oversight of the WAPP Information and Coordination Centre. The existence of such a center from an early stage in the development of the market is an important step, one that mirrors the creation of the SAPP Coordination Centre in Harare.

Having a codified regional transmission tariff methodology (RTTM) provides a clear basis for utilities to start to evaluate the financial benefits of trading electricity and the costs of wheeling power to which they will be exposed. It also ensures that the TSOs that provide wheeling services can be assured that their costs will be recoverable. This includes not only the investment costs associated with the transmission assets used for power wheeling, but also the operation and maintenance costs and the costs of losses.

Learnings from the Lao PDR–Thailand–Malaysia–Singapore Power Interchange Project (LTMS-PIP)

The first phase of the LTMS-PIP project is an important example to consider in relation to the expansion of power trading in the GMS, because it is representative of the type of trading that is envisaged in the Stage 2 model defined in MoU-2 and the "Scenario 2" trading (see Chapter 1). The key elements of the project which have potential application elsewhere include

- the integration of commercial arrangements for power sales and wheeling into a tripartite agreement involving the buyer, the seller, and the wheeling service provider. For the short-term development of power trading in the GMS, bilateral contracts that can be entered into readily will be essential, and having contractual structures and examples that make this possible will be highly beneficial. Phase 1 of LTMS-PIP provides a useful precedent for further consideration by GMS countries;
- the definition of wheeling within the Energy Purchase and Wheeling Agreement (EPWA) is wide enough to recover all the key costs to which Electricity Generating Authority of Thailand (EGAT), as the wheeling utility, is exposed. This includes:
  (i) a MW-mile approach to the recovery of the costs of transmission assets;
  (ii) losses charges based on simulation of the import and export of the proposed 100 MW power transfer and taking account of the system marginal price in Thailand;

(iii) balancing charges to make good of any shortfall in the energy delivered from the Lao PDR into Thailand and exported from Thailand into Malaysia (either in-kind or via cash settlement); and
(iv) the recovery of an appropriate level of administration charges.[5]

Balancing Arrangements: International Comparisons

Table 6 presents a comparison of international approaches to balancing arrangements, demonstrating how the proposed solution for the GMS has been developed based on international best practice.

Table 6: Comparison of International Balancing Mechanisms

	Continental Europe	Nordic	US	SAPP	GCC	GMS (proposal)
Providers of balancing services	Operating reserves from control areas plus reserve sharing between control areas	Operating reserves from a common stack	Operating reserves from control areas plus reserve sharing between control areas	Operating reserves from control areas	Operating reserves from control areas	Operating reserves from control areas plus reserve sharing between control areas
AGC and ACE control	Yes	No because it is a single control area	Yes	Yes	Yes, but not a requirement in rules	Yes
Measurement of imbalances	Actual schedule for all parties	Actual schedule for all parties	N/A for NY, PJM, & NE; CAISO calculates balance and imbalance energy separately	Actual schedule for all parties	Actual schedule for all parties	Actual schedule for all parties
Inadvertent energy	No	No	Yes, but should be small if NERC criteria are met	25 MWh per hour	50 MWh per hour	No
Imbalance metering interval	15 mins	1 hour	5-10 minutes	1 hour	1 hour	1 hour
Price setting mechanism	Balancing bids and offers	Balancing bids and offers	5-minute market bids and offers	DA market clearing price	OCGT marginal price	Marginal unit type costs

continued on next page

[5] Electricity Generating Authority of Thailand. *Future Cross-Border Trade and the ASEAN Power Grid.* http://www.appp.or.th/imgadmins/document/09105940.pdf.

Table 6 *continued*

	Continental Europe	Nordic	US	SAPP	GCC	GMS (proposal)
Imbalance price marginal vs average	Weighted average & marginal	Weighted average	Marginal	Marginal	N/A	Marginal
Penalties for out-of-balance	No	No	NY, PJM, & NE: No. CAISO: Yes	Yes	No	Possibly
Control area performance measured	No	No	Yes: NERC CPS1, BAAL, and DCS1	Yes: NERC CPS1, CPS2, and DCS1	No	Yes: NERC CPS1, CPS2, and DCS1
Penalties for control area non-performance	No	No	Yes	Yes	No	Possibly

ACE = Area Control Error; AGC = Automatic Generation Control; BAAL = Balancing Authority ACE Limit; CAISO = California Independent System Operator; CPS = Control Performance Standard; DA = day-ahead; DCS = Disturbance Control Standard; GCC = Gulf Coordination Council; GMS = Greater Mekong Subregion; NE = New England; NERC = North American Electric Reliability Corporation; NY = New York; OCGT = Open Cycle Gas Turbine; PJM = Pennsylvania-New Jersey-Maryland electricity market; SAPP = Southern African Power Pool; US = United States.

Source: Ricardo Energy & Environment.

8.3 Recommendations

To provide the foundations for increased power trading in the GMS, a series of measures are proposed:

- the regulatory, technical, and commercial measures required to give **open access** to the power networks in the GMS—for generators and IPPs that wish to export power to neighbouring countries using the transmission network in their own country;
- a **methodology for wheeling charges** that will enable transmission owners and system operators to recover a proportion of the capital costs, operation and maintenance costs, and losses associated with hosting wheeling power flows (i.e., power flows arising from electricity trades from which they do not benefit as buyers or sellers of electricity);
- a set of **short-term bilateral trading rules** that enables trades to be more flexible than the current case of using long-term bilateral PPAs. This includes proposals for identifying the technical feasibility of trades, and a simplified process for willing buyers and sellers to identify and enter into potential trades;
- a **balancing mechanism** that permits initially the “in-kind” settlement of imbalances, and as an alternative for later development, a cash-based process.

A key finding from this study is the need for a regional GMS Regional Power Coordination Centre or market operator that can take responsibility for:

- coordinating the planning of regional interconnections;
- calculating wheeling charges and transmission losses associated with regional power trading;

- publishing potential short-term bilateral trades and undertaking the technical and commercial processes required to assess ATC on the transmission systems to support short-term bilateral trades;
- carrying out calculations in support of the settlement of inadvertent energy transfers (balancing), involving the collection and processing of meter data; and
- potentially in the future, acting as an agent to facilitate financial settlement of power trades.

These functions represent a significant extension of the current role of the RPTCC and should be discussed by the RPTCC members to agree on a suitable organization to fulfill these functions.

All of the above conclusions and the associated background work are documented in full in the series of reports that have been produced under ADB's technical assistance TA8830-REG Harmonizing the Grater Mekong Sub-region Power Systems to Facilitate Regional Power Trade.[6] The principles presented in this study aims to inform future work in engaging with electricity industry stakeholders regionally and expanding regional power trade.

[6] https://www.adb.org/projects/documents/reg-harmonizing-gms-power-systems-to-facilitate-regional-power-trade-tar.

Appendix 1: International Case Studies

A1.1 The Southern African Power Pool

Southern Africa has an abundance of commercial energy resources but they are not evenly distributed. To minimize the cost of supply, the promotion of regional cooperation is vital; and integration of national networks was identified as a move that could enhance reliability and ensure security of supply for all. This led to a number of cross border interconnections and inter-utility connections being developed. Through cross-border connections, utilities have managed to avoid or delay investments in power generation infrastructure, reduce operating costs, and increase reliability benefits.

In many parts of the world (especially the US and Europe), regional power trade arrangements started with simple interconnections between neighbouring utilities. Such interconnections were used by utilities initially to manage emergency situations. In some cases, the interconnected network developed into a more sophisticated formal legal platform where different stakeholders shared responsibilities for system operation and market regulation. The main cost saving in such an arrangement came from economies of scale achieved through combined operations and sharing new interconnector capacity.

Early Trade in Southern Africa

Cooperation and interconnections in the Southern African region started in the 1950s with the construction of a transmission line between Nseke in the Democratic Republic of Congo (DRC) and Kitwe in Zambia. This line was established in 1958 to supply electricity to a copper mine in Zambia. In the 1960s, construction of Kariba dam was completed, after which the interconnection between Zambia and Zimbabwe was established. In 1975, an interconnection between South Africa and Mozambique was established through a high voltage direct current (HVDC) transmission line. This line was constructed to link Hidroeléctrica de Cahora Bassa (2,400 megawatts) in Mozambique with the Apollo substation in Johannesburg, South Africa.

In 1992, the region experienced a drought, and this resulted in severe electricity shortages because many of hydropower plants in the region were not able to supply adequately. This shortage highlighted the need to formalize regional power cooperation. As mentioned before, the commercial energy resources of the Southern African region are unevenly distributed and cross-border electricity exchange is very important for economic development. The region has very large reserves of low-cost hydropower in the northern part (in the DRC and Zambia) and large reserves of cheap coal deposits in the southern parts (in South Africa, Botswana, and Mozambique).

Establishment of SAPP through Inter-Government Memorandum of Understanding, 1995

The Southern African Power Pool (SAPP) was created in August 1995 when majority of member countries of the Southern African Development Community (SADC), signed an Inter-Government Memorandum of Understanding (MoU). The main purpose behind this MoU was to establish SAPP and pronounce the clear intentions of the signatories to enhance regional power cooperation.

Table A1.1 states the names of 12 SAPP member countries and their respective national utilities.

Table A1.1: Southern African Power Pool Member Countries and National Utilities

Country	National Utility	Country	National Utility
Angola	Empresa Nacional de Electricidade	Mozambique	Electricidade de Moçambique
Botswana	Botswana Power Corporation	Namibia	NamPower
DRC	Société Nationale d'Electricité	South Africa	Electricity Supply Commission
Lesotho	Lesotho Electricity Supply Commission	Swaziland	Swaziland Electricity Board
Malawi	Electricity Supply Commission	Tanzania	Tanzania Electricity Supply Company
Zambia	Zambia Electricity Supply Corporation	Zimbabwe	Zimbabwe Electricity Supply Authority

DRC = Democratic Republic of Congo.

Source: Ricardo Energy & Environment.

Inter-Utility Memorandum of Understanding, 1995

Also in 1995, an Inter-Utility MoU was signed by various vertically integrated (state-owned) utilities of the SADC. At this point, membership regarding SAPP was limited to the national utilities of the member countries.

Agreement between Operating Members, 1995

The main purpose behind this agreement was to establish the basic principles and rules under which the interconnected members could operate. This document provides information on:

- membership,
- rights and obligation of the Operating Members,
- SAPP Operating Sub- Committee,
- SAPP Coordination Centre,
- accredited capacity obligation,
- Service Schedules, and
- metering.

SAPP Operating Guidelines, 1995

The SAPP Operating Guidelines established in August 1995 were developed to ensure that SAPP members operate the interconnected Southern African network effectively and efficiently. The document provided guidelines in six key areas (Table A1.2). All interconnected utilities were asked to comply with this document and use it to develop more guidelines that will govern the operation of each individual network. Also, these operating guidelines were based on those used by the North American Electric Reliability Council (NERC), and all members were asked to monitor their operations and compare them against a benchmark.

Table A1.2: Summary of Southern African Power Pool Operating Guidelines

Guideline 1: System Control • Generation Control • Voltage Control • Time and Frequency Control • Interchange Scheduling • Control Performance Criteria • Inadvertent Energy Management • Control Surveys • Control Equipment **Guideline 2: System Security** • Active Power (MW) Supply • Reactive Power (MVAR) Supply • Transmission Operation • Relay Coordination • Monitoring Interconnection Parameters • Information Exchange – Normal System Conditions • Information Exchange – Disturbance Reporting • Maintenance	**Guideline 3: Emergency Operations** • Insufficient Generation Capacity • Transmission – Overload, Voltage Control • Load Shedding • System Restoration • Emergency Information Exchange • Special System or Control Area Action • Control Centre Back-Up **Guideline 4: Operating Personnel** • Responsibility and Authority • Selection • Training • Responsibility to Other Operating Groups **Guideline 5: Operations Planning** • Normal Operations • Planning for Short-Term Emergency Conditions • Planning for Long-Term Emergency Conditions • Load Shedding and System Restoration	**Guidelines 6: Telecommunications** • Facilities • System Controller Telecommunication Procedures • Loss of Telecommunications

MVAR = mega volt amps (reactive), MW = megawatt.

Source: Ricardo Energy & Environment.

Initial Years with Bilateral Contracts

During the initial years of SAPP, members were locked into long-term, high load factor, firm bilateral contracts for security of supply and other captive sales reasons. Eskom, the South African electricity public utility, was the major supplier to many countries. The Société Nationale D'électricité (SNEL) of the DRC; the ZESCO Ltd (formerly known as Zambia Electricity Supply Corporation Limited) of Zambia; and the Electricidade de Moçambique (EDM) and the Hidroeléctrica de Cahora Bassa (HCB) of Mozambique were net exporters. During this period, the major buyers were those countries that could not meet their peak demand: Zimbabwe Electricity Supply Authority (ZESA), Botswana Power Corporation (BPC), NamPower (national power utility company of Namibia), Lesotho Electricity Company (PTY) LTD LEC, and Swaziland Electricity Company (SEC).

During the initial years of a power pool, countries with surplus generation usually supply the countries with deficit through bilateral contracts. Even today the majority of trade in SAPP is undertaken through bilateral contracts, and the importers supply portfolios that include firm and non-firm bilateral contracts from various suppliers. For example, BPC could have long-term firm bilateral contracts with Eskom; medium-term bilateral contracts with Eskom, EDM, SNEL, and ZESCO (firm and non-firm); and short-term bilateral contracts with NamPower, Eskom, ZESA, and EDM. Contracts could incorporate right of first refusal clauses.

Revised Inter-Government Memorandum of Understanding, 2006

In this MoU, it had been agreed that there was a need for all participants to:

- coordinate and cooperate with others in planning, development, and operation of their power system. Such efforts would minimize cost and all stakeholders would be able to maintain reliability, autonomy, and self-sufficiency to the degree they desire;
- fully recover cost and share the resulting benefits from the required reduction in generation capacity, less use of fossil fuels, and enhanced use of hydropower sources; and
- coordinate and cooperate with others in planning, development, and operation of a regional electricity market based on the requirements of various SADC members.

Defining Authorities Responsible for Implementation. Each party that had signed the treaty was asked to designate person/s who would be responsible for implementing its obligation under the MoU. Those assigned should consult with each other to resolve any problems that may arise from implementation of the MoU.

Defining Authorities for Participation. In the MoU, all parties acknowledge that all national power utilities and other electric supply enterprises could participate as members of SAPP.[1] Such participation would be subject to the respective domestic laws, approval by the SAPP Executive Committee, and terms and conditions as stipulated by SAPP. All parties were advised to refrain from passing any legislation or administrative measure that could prevent participation of SAPP members. Any inclusion of electricity supply enterprises from non-member states in SAPP shall be allowed after approval of the parties.

Dispute Resolution. The MoU also stated that any disputes that arise between two or more parties from the application of the revised MoU could not be settled amicably and shall be resolved through the SADC Tribunal.

Revised Inter-Utility Memorandum of Understanding, 2005

The first Inter-Utility MoU was signed in December 1995; and in 1995–2005, various national power utilities had started the process of restructuring. Hence, there was a strong desire that the participation in SAPP by entities other than the national power utilities should be formally recognized. The main purposes behind this revised Inter-Utility MoU were

- to encourage participants to coordinate and cooperate in the planning, development, and operation of the regional electricity market based on the requirements of the member states;

[1] Electricity supply enterprise include power utilities, independent power producers, independent transmission companies, and service providers.

- to ensure that every member is provided with rights and obligations to own or provide the facilities required to provide electricity services. This shall be regardless of the size or type of organization;
- to provide an opportunity to all electric supply enterprises situated in the SADC to become members of the SAPP;
- to allow the SAPP Executive Committee to admit any electric supply enterprises from the nonmember states of SAPP. This shall be subject to the provisions of the Inter-Governmental MoU and approval of SADC;
- to allow the SAPP Management Committee to grant the following status:
  (i) **Observer Status.** Electricity supply enterprise interested in the interconnected operation of the pool
  (ii) **Affiliate Status.** Any organization interested in the activities of the SAPP
  (iii) **Participation Status.** Entity interconnected to the SAPP grid and interested in the operation of SAPP and
- to update the management structure of SAPP and the roles and responsibilities of each subcommittee.

Comparison with Memorandums of Understanding in the Greater Mekong Subregion

A comparison has been made between the coverage of the SAPP Inter-Utility Memorandum of Understanding (2007) and the Memorandum of Understanding on the Guidelines for the Implementation of the Regional Power Trade Operating Agreement Stage 1. The results of this comparison are summarized below.

This comparison demonstrates that there is considerably more detail provided in the SAPP MoU than is the case with the GMS version, and that there are some gaps that need to be filled for the GMS through additional documentation.

The most significant differences between SAPP and the GMS are as follows:

- There is a hierarchy of documentation in SAPP comprising an Agreement between Operating Members and a set of Operating Guidelines, which govern the operating arrangements for trading between member utilities. These documents, or equivalent, will be required once further trading in the GMS begins.
- SAPP has a clear organization structure defined beneath the Management Committee (see Figure A1.1), consisting of subcommittees and the Coordination Centre. In the case of the GMS, a subset of these functions are intended to be fulfilled by a number of working groups, including a Focal Group and a Planning Working Group (PWG), which initially have the functions of both the Operational Planning Working Group (OPWG) and the System Planning Working Group (SPWG). These working groups will have an important role in fulfilling several recommendations in this report, and clarification of their roles is required as they work on market implementation alongside the WGRI and the WGPG.
- The SAPP MoU is far less restrictive than the GMS MoU regarding membership of the electricity companies. The Greater Mekong Subregion Memorandum of Understanding on the Guidelines for the Implementation of the Regional Power Trade Operating Agreement Stage 1: "The Executive Authorities that shall be entitled by the Government of the GMS member countries to perform the cross-border power trade among the GMS member countries and

carry out all the actions needed to achieve it are the entities responsible for the generation scheduling and the supervision and control of the operations of the transmission system of each of the countries involved in the trade (referred as the Transmission System Operators), namely the Electricité du Cambodge (EDC), the China Southern Power Grid Co. Ltd (CSG), the Electricité du Laos (EDL), the Myanmar Electric Power Enterprise (MEPE), the EGAT Public Company Limited, and the Viet Nam Electricity (EVN)."

- This implies that the transmission system operators (TSOs) in each country are the entities permitted to undertake power trading. The MoU will therefore require amendments if either IPPs or international traders are to be permitted to participate in regional trading.
- Both MoUs contain provisions for dispute resolution; however, the SAPP MoU makes the SAPP Coordination Centre responsible for managing the dispute resolution process. The GMS MoU makes this process the responsibility of the affected TSOs, and refers to the possibility of involving international arbitration if an agreement cannot be reached between them. If the RPTCC were to take a more central role in dispute resolution, this would align more closely with the clarity achieved in the SAPP MoU. For an efficient dispute resolution in the electricity sector, it is important to ensure that responsibility for running the process is clearly allocated to one body, and this is particularly the case in regional electricity markets, where communications between countries and across regulatory jurisdictions are needed.

Figure A1.1: Management Structure of the Southern African Power Pool

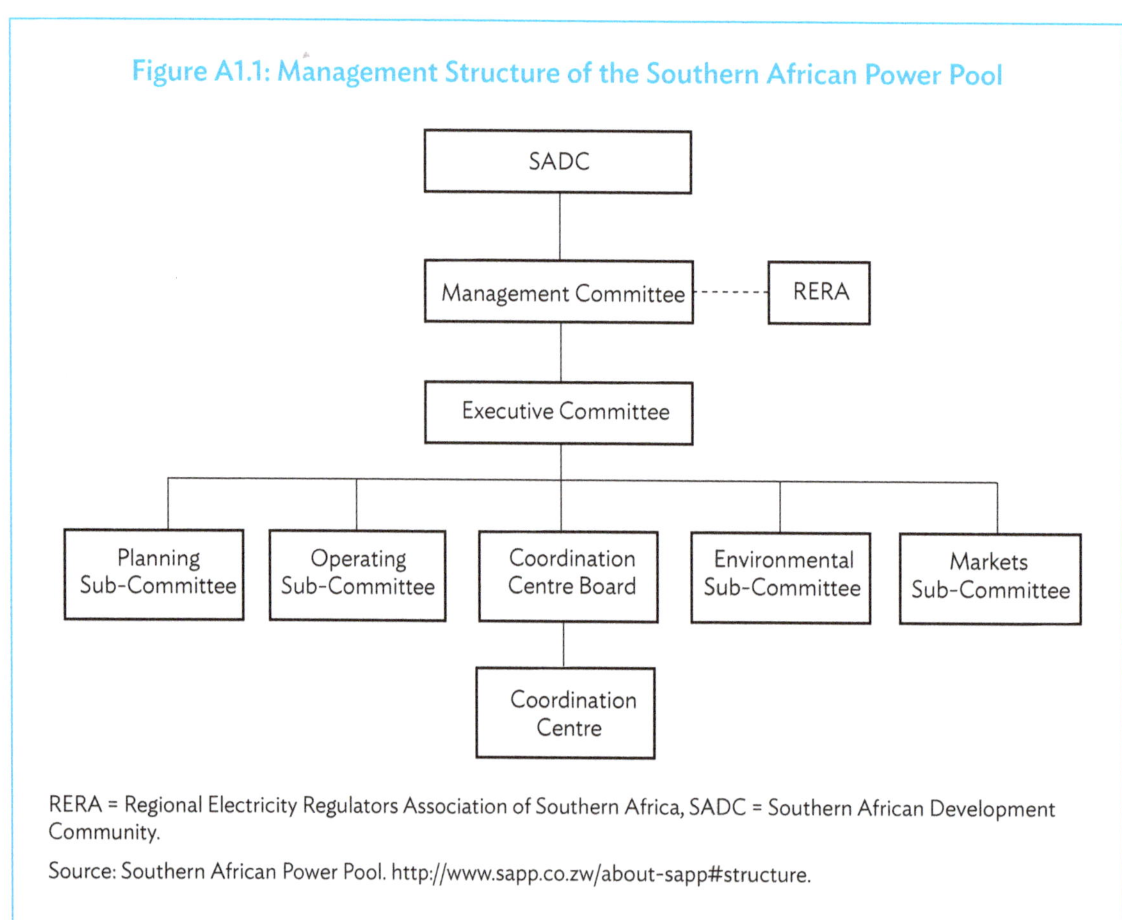

RERA = Regional Electricity Regulators Association of Southern Africa, SADC = Southern African Development Community.

Source: Southern African Power Pool. http://www.sapp.co.zw/about-sapp#structure.

Revised Agreement between Operating Members, 2008

The 1995 agreement between operating members of SAPP was revised in May 2008. This document provides the basic principles and rules under which the interconnected portion of the SAPP network will operate.

The agreement between operating members provides rules and principles for determining rate mechanisms for mandatory services such as emergency support, wheeling, scheduled outage energy, transmission losses, and control area services.

The revised agreement provides information about the functions, reporting structures and cost of SAPP Coordination Centre, accredited capacity obligations, metering, settlements, and dispute resolution.

All-Party Access to Transmission

In SAPP, all parties have access to the available wheeling capacity. An independent power producer (IPP) in Mozambique could potentially sell power to a utility in Namibia and this would require wheeling power through South Africa's (Eskom) network.

For the initial trading in the GMS, it is recommended that either national single buyer organizations, which may be the TSOs, or separately identified international trader organizations, coordinate international trades entered into by IPPs. Specific arrangements will be required, however, for IPPs that are not interconnected with their national transmission networks, and that wish to trade using the cross-border transmission assets associated with another IPP's generating plant.

The availability of wheeling capacity is determined under SAPP market operating rules to give priority to allocating transmission infrastructure to firm bilateral contracts and non-firm bilateral contracts before providing any capacity to competitive market transactions. Similar arrangements should be proposed in the market rules for the initial trading in the GMS.

Wheeling Arrangements

SAPP started with a wheeling charge of 7.5 % of the value of the energy wheeled through a third-party transmission system. If two wheelers were involved in the transaction, then the wheeling charge would be 15 % of the value of the energy wheeled.

In a refinement to this methodology, a MW-km method was adopted under which the wheeling charge applicable through a third-party network is related to:

- the proportion of the country's network capacity used (based on thermal rating),
- the age of the assets and current replacement cost of the asset, and
- allowance for the operational and maintenance cost of assets involved in wheeling.

The wheeling charge is paid by the purchaser of energy. The seller of the electricity is responsible of making good out of the additional losses imposed on the wheeler's transmission network. Power system analysis software could be used to calculate losses on an hourly basis. The new wheeling charges were phased over a period of 3 years. The transaction charges are nondirectional and do not give credits for superimposition of transactions that could potentially reduce the flows on the line.

The SAPP carried out a comprehensive study on the possibilities of applying a more sophisticated wheeling charge structure to accommodate the introduction of a day-ahead spot market, in which specific counterparties to trades would not necessarily be identified. In this situation, a simple structure of "entry and exit" charges would be required, relating only to the location entry of buyers or sellers from or to the centralized power pool. This more complex pricing structure is still under consideration and has yet to be introduced.

From Cooperative Pool to Competitive Pool

Through bilateral contracts, the utilities engaged in a continuous exchange of base load energy with other resources such as emergency support and spinning reserves.

In 2000, when SAPP was preparing for competitive trade, some of the bilateral contracts had to be renegotiated to pave the way for competition. Trade volumes, conditions, and to some extent, prices, were renegotiated, and the trade portfolios of the members changed. Some traditional net importers could also export in certain trade windows. For example, ZESA could have long-term firm bilateral import contracts with Eskom; medium-term bilateral import contracts with Eskom, EDM, SNEL, and ZESCO (firm and non-firm); and short-term bilateral export contracts with BPC and NamPower. In addition, some right of first refusal clauses began to disappear.

The precursor to the SAPP Day-Ahead Market (DAM) and the short-term energy market (STEM) was established in 2001 to create competition in the SAPP electricity trading market. It was based on suppliers and buyers submit their bids to the SAPP Coordination Centre, where a market to match supply and demand based on prices could be run; and the results as to who is matched to who and at what price were published. Successful matches formed short-term contracts for transaction the following day. All participants knew the cleared transactions and their prices. There was no confidentiality.

Immediate benefits included price drops, improved trade efficiency as importers found windows in which to export, significantly increased trade volumes, and large financial savings in power purchases. However, the trading platform was not perfect; and in 2009, a more sophisticated DAM platform succeeded it using NordPool donor funding and expertise (the platform was upgraded in 2013/2014).

The SAPP market began moving toward a coordinated system dispatch, which involves:

- continuous matching of supply and demand;
- maintaining system power quality and reliable operation of assets; and
- helping and coordinating power transactions between various interconnected systems.

To maintain higher levels of reliability, the overall transmission network could be divided into control areas. A control area is expected to meet and continuously match its resources with its load. In many power pools, countries continue to ensure that their own internal generation plus imports/exports are continuously balanced. To save cost, utilities or countries may decide to form a single control area and such a process constitutes a form of "central dispatch." Centralized dispatched power systems are expected to achieve higher levels of efficiency; as such, a dispatch center would have larger mix of generators, and could better coordinate maintenance of units or reserves.[2]

[2] A highly sophisticated form of control area balancing is practiced in Europe, and this formed the basis of the recommendations for the future evolution of the market in the GMS, as recommended in the report: ADB. 2010. *Facilitating Regional Power Trading and Environmentally Sustainable Development of Electricity Infrastructure in the Greater Mekong Subregion.* Manila. https://www.adb.org/projects/41018-012/main

In SAPP, imports and exports are scheduled by hour for the day ahead through a control area operator who uses automatic generation control (AGC). All SAPP members belong to one of the three control areas (ZESCO, ZESA, and Eskom). Every TSO submits its import/export schedules to its host control area operator, who then includes them in the AGC aggregated with others and the host's own schedule.

Generally, domestic supply takes precedence to any wheeling transaction. However, some complex contracts come with protective clauses.

Established during the deficit period, the DAM had a slow start. There was no power to trade and where little power was available, the transmission wheeling paths were congested with bilateral contracts, which also suffered curtailments. As the deficit situation began to lift from 2012, trade volumes had increased. The DAM platform has a more sophisticated price determination methodology (based on market clearing principles) and congestion management methodologies that send accurate investor signals; and the platform manages the trade, reconciliation, and settlement processes centrally, and faster. Matched participants are only known to the market operator.

Table A1.3: Southern African Power Pool Market Clearing Prices

Market Clearing Price, 2016–2017	
Month	**Average MCP (USc/kWh)**
Apr-2016	8.53
May	7.86
Jun	9.32
Jul	9.69
Aug	9.97
Sep	9.17
Oct	6.31
Nov	6.50
Dec	5.55
Jan-2017	5.34
Feb	4.74
Mar	3.78
Average	**7.23**

USc/kWh = United States cents per kilowatthour.

Source: Southern African Power Pool. 2017. *Annual Report 2017*. p. 28. http://www.sapp.co.zw/sites/default/files/SAPP.pdf.

In 2016, additional trading platforms were introduced, comprising a Forward Physical Month-Ahead Market (FPM-M), a Forward Physical Weekly Market (FPM-W), and an IntraDay Market (IDM). The total volume of trades matched on the competitive market in 2016 had increased compared with that of 2015; however, the volume of the trades that could be successfully completed was significantly lower than the volume matched (63% of the energy matched in the competitive markets in 2016/2017 could not be traded as a result of constraints on the transmission network).[3]

According to the 2017 SAPP annual report, on average, 8 out of 13 interconnected members have been active in the competitive market.

Unlike the bilateral trade in which the prices and conditions are confidential, the competitive market prices are published for members on a daily basis. Market clearing prices (MCPs) for 2016/2017 were slightly lower than those of the previous year. The average MCP for 2016/2017 was **7.23 US cents per kilowatt hour (USc/kWh)** which is slightly lower than the **8.31 USc/kWh** recorded the previous year. Recent SAPP market clearing prices are summarized in Table A1.3.

[3] Southern African Power Pool. 2017. *Annual Report 2017*.p. 25. http://www.sapp.co.zw/sites/default/files/SAPP.pdf.

Competitive Trade alongside Bilateral Trade

In the SAPP financial year 2016/2017, the competitive market share of electricity trade in the region was 11%. The balance of trade (89%) was carried out on the bilateral market. Table A1.4 compares the market of trade in bilateral and competitive markets. Without the transmission constraints, it is estimated that the market could immediately grow to 35% of total trade in SAPP.

Table A1.4: Market Share of Bilateral and Competitive Trade, 2016–2017

Month	Traded Bilaterally (MWh)	Energy Traded on Market (MWh)	Competitive Market Share (Actual - %)	Energy Matched on Market (MWh)	Competitive Market Share (Potential - %)
Apr-2016	782,194	47,067	5.68	117,802	15.06
May	745,676	40,538	5.16	94,174	12.63
Jun	501,222	30,878	5.80	219,077	43.71
Jul	799,550	47,792	5.64	227,386	28.44
Aug	680,633	118,412	14.82	285,082	41.88
Sep	753,297	109,612	12.70	457,257	60.70
Oct	705,944	132,219	15.77	356,073	50.44
Nov	789,597	140,129	15.07	473,567	59.98
Dec	594,293	111,596	15.81	226,744	38.15
Jan-2017	551,489	87,400	13.68	128,443	23.29
Feb	521,796	82,535	13.66	101,603	19.47
Mar	565,925	74,878	11.69	92,564	16.36
Totals	**7,991,616**	**1,023,056**	**11.35**	**2,779,772**	**34.78**

MWh = megawatt hour.

Source: Southern African Power Pool. 2017. *Annual Report 2017.* Harare.

Lessons from the Southern African Power Pool

Market evolution

The evolution of the SAPP market has taken place through a series of separate steps, with increasing sophistication.

- The market began with a simple structure of **long-term bilateral contracts**.
- These were supported by a variant of **postage-stamp wheeling charges**.
- The market was extended to include a **short-term market** based on a bulletin board offering day-ahead trading options. A **balancing mechanism** was introduced at the same time to facilitate financial settlement of imbalances.
- A more sophisticated **day-ahead** trading platform was then introduced, based on sophisticated market clearing and zonal prices, signalling congestion in the transmission system.

- Additional **month-ahead, week-ahead**, and **intra-day** platforms have recently been added to increase the flexibility and options available to market participants.

This evolutionary approach, implemented over a period of 20 years, has enabled market participants to grow in their confidence and understanding of the market.

Structure and organization

The structure and organization of the SAPP market has relied on several key high-level agreements:

- an Inter-Government MoU, setting down the high-level principles of international cooperation in electricity sector planning and energy trading;
- an Inter-Utility MoU, governing the operational arrangements between the power utilities themselves;
- an Agreement between Operating Members, governing the rights and responsibilities of the members and the regional organization, including the SAPP Executive Committee, Management Committee, and Coordination Centre; and
- the SAPP Operating Guidelines, covering many of the technical areas of cooperation that would otherwise be covered by a regional grid code.

The existing GMS MoU-1 and MoU-2 documents set down some of the high-level provisions that the countries have agreed to comply with regarding market development. It is recommended that a similar set of documents to those in items ii–iv (above) from the SAPP market are developed within the GMS—to implement a set of practical measures and assist the development of inter-utility cooperation and regional trading.

Another recommendation is the establishment of the Regional Power Coordination Centre in the GMS as a regional coordinating body, fulfilling a similar role to the SAPP Coordination Centre.

Constitution of the Working Group on Regulating Issues and the Working Group on Performance Standards and Grid Codes

In order to enable the WGRI and the WGPG to take on a broader remit, it is recommended that they be established as subcommittees rather than working groups of the RPTCC. This would mirror more accurately the structure that has successfully been implemented in the SAPP and potentially give these bodies greater authority to match the responsibilities attached to their role.

A1.2 The West African Power Pool

The West African Power Pool (WAPP) came into being in 1999 following a decision taken at the 22nd Summit of the Economic Community of West African States (ECOWAS) Authority of Heads of State and Government. A later summit (2006), adopted the Articles of Agreement defining the WAPP organization and its functions.

The overall **vision** of WAPP is "to integrate the national power systems into a unified regional electricity market with the ultimate goal of providing in the medium and long term, a regular and reliable energy at competitive cost to the citizenry of the ECOWAS region"; its **mission** is "to promote and develop power generation and transmission infrastructures as well as to [coordinate] power exchange amongst the ECOWAS Member States."[4]

[4] West African Power Pool. http://www.ecowapp.org/en/content/creation-wapp.

ECOWAS comprises 15 member states: Benin, Burkina Faso, Cabo Verde, Côte d'Ivoire, The Gambia, Ghana, Guinea, Guinea Bissau, Liberia, Mali, Niger, Nigeria, Senegal, Sierra Leone, and Togo.

The governance structure of WAPP is similar to SAPP in that it comprises a combination of high-level management bodies and lower-level operating committees.

The highest-level WAPP management body is the General Assembly, which has representation from the 29 utilities that are members of WAPP.

Beneath the General Assembly is the Executive Board. This is the body that has executive responsibility for implementing the decisions taken by the General Assembly. The Executive Board comprises 13 members who are directors general or managing directors/chief executive officers of the ECOWAS national power utilities, a secretary general, and an honorary member.

The Executive Board oversees the work of five organizational committees, and the committees are responsible for undertaking specific technical functions and advising the Executive Board on policy matters. The five organizational committees comprise the

- Engineering and Operations Committee,
- Strategic Planning and Environment Committee,
- Finance Committee,
- Human Resource and Governance Committee, and
- Distribution and Commercial Committee.

Additionally, a General Secretariat fulfills the core central administrative functions. The General Secretariat comprises three departments, including the

- Department of Information and Coordination Centre,
- Department of Administration and Finance, and
- Department of Planning, Investments Programming and Environmental Safeguards.

The WAPP organizational structure is shown in Figure A1.2.

WAPP Articles of Agreement

The Articles of Agreement lays down the high-level provisions that determine the structure and organization of WAPP, including the functions of the General Assembly and the Executive Board, together with the arrangements for leadership and functioning of the different organizational committees. They also stipulate the role of the General Secretariat and the Information and Coordination Centre, which is the focal point of coordination and information provision for the WAPP members.

Arrangements for the financing of WAPP's activities and the procedures for resolving disputes between members are also described in the agreement.

Figure A1.2: Organizational Structure of the West African Power Pool

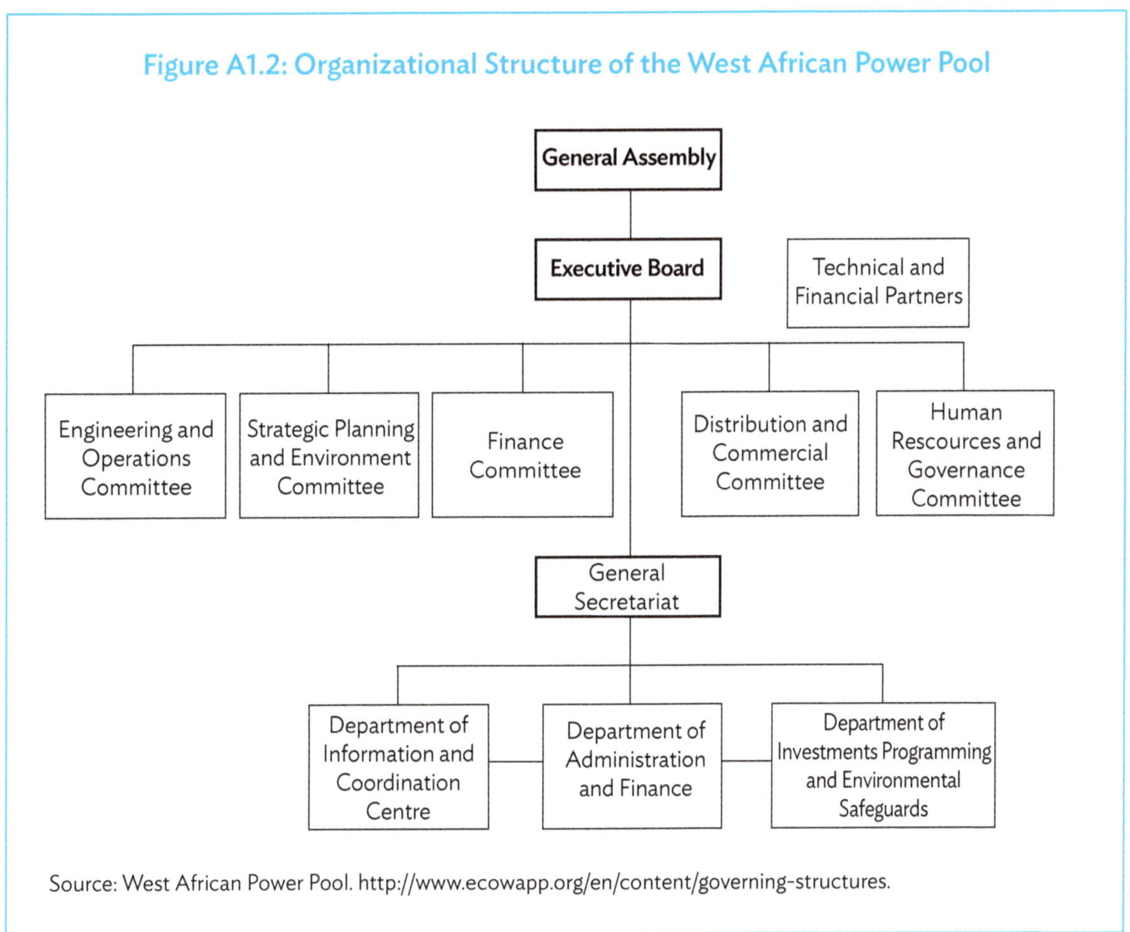

Source: West African Power Pool. http://www.ecowapp.org/en/content/governing-structures.

Regional Market Rules

A set of Regional Market Rules (RMR) for the WAPP was approved by the ECOWAS Regional Electricity Regulatory Authority (ERERA) in August 2015. The RMR sets out the basis for regional electricity trading to develop in three phases. Phase 1 provisions include

- trading that is currently negotiated on "case by case" basis to be standardized under the oversight of the WAPP System and Market Operator (SMO);
- trade is based on bilateral agreements between neighbouring countries;
- model bilateral agreements are to be used for trading, covering short-, medium-, and long-term arrangements;
- transmission pricing is agreed between the trading parties, pending the adoption of a new Regional Transmission Pricing Methodology;
- trading is to be carried out in accordance with the RMR, and trading carried out under the rules of Phase 1 should not be prevented by the evolution to Phase 2 of the RMR; and
- ERERA, as the regional regulatory body, is responsible for enforcing the RMR and for settling disputes between market participants.

Phase 2 of the market represents an extension of the Phase 1 rules, and covers:

- bilateral trading taking place through the networks of third countries (i.e., power wheeling is enabled using standard contracts);
- short-term trading which will be possible through a day-ahead market;
- a regulated transmission pricing regime for regional trades that is overseen by ERERA; and
- a fully operational SMO for the region.

Phase 3 of the regional market is a very long-term potential development, and would include:

- operation of a fully competitive market, which would have sufficient liquidity, and involve a significant level of competition. This would require the availability of significantly increased transmission capacity between countries and adequate reserve margins to enable trading without jeopardizing the system security; and
- potential integration of other products into the market, including ancillary services trading, and the potential introduction of financial contracts trading rather than trades based solely on physical contracts.

At this stage, detailed market rules are provided only for the first phase of the market.

Regional Regulatory Body

The role of ERERA is significant in the oversight of the regional market; and while there are structures within WAPP to facilitate the operation of the market and the agreement of trading principles between the market participants, the enforcement of the RMR rests with an external body. This is different from the approach adopted in SAPP and that proposed for the GMS, wherein it is not proposed that a regional regulatory body with enforcing powers be introduced. In SAPP, the market is overseen by the Executive Committee, the Management Committee, and the Coordination Centre, and so, in common with many markets internationally, is effectively self-regulating, with rule changes requiring only the approval of the market members themselves.

The overarching framework of the ECOWAS Energy Protocol agreed by the member states of ECOWAS provided the context for the creation of ERERA. The main functions of ERERA are to

- regulate cross-border interconnections and trading arrangements,
- define transparent tariff arrangements for regional power pool trades,
- provide a framework of technical and economic regulation for the development of the regional market,
- provide policy advice to ECOWAS member states on energy issues, and
- provide a forum for dispute resolution between regional market participants.

Regional Interconnections in WAPP

A major constraint on the development of WAPP as a regional market is the extent of power system interconnection in the West African region.

The WAPP 2016–2019 Business Plan states the following:

"...the Business Plan shall strive to ensure that all 14 mainland ECOWAS Member States shall be completely interconnected within the period."[5]

This goal will be an essential step forward to enabling trade to increase beyond the very limited levels currently taking place.

The business plan incorporates five key objectives:

- update the ECOWAS master plan for generation and transmission;
- implement the WAPP priority projects identified in the previous master plan;
- establish the regional energy market in accordance with the RMR;
- implement the WAPP "Dark Fibre" project, to utilize spare fibre optic communications capacity;
- conduct capacity building activities for the Secretariat workforce to raise performance standards in the WAPP organization.

The priority interconnection projects for WAPP are centered around the following key initiatives:

- Coastal Transmission Backbone Subprogram (Côte d'Ivoire, Ghana, Benin/Togo, Nigeria)
- Inter-zonal Transmission Hub Sub-program (Burkina Faso, Senegal River Basin System via Mali, Mali via Côte d'Ivoire, Liberia-Sierra Leone-Guinea via Côte d'Ivoire)
- North-Core Transmission Sub-program (Nigeria, Niger, Burkina Faso, Benin)
- OMVG/OMVS Power System Development Subprogram (The Gambia, Guinea, Guinea Bissau, Mali, Senegal)
- Côte d'Ivoire-Liberia-Sierra Leone-Guinea Power System Redevelopment Subprogram (Côte d'Ivoire, Liberia, Sierra Leone, Guinea).

Current Levels of Trading in WAPP

The current levels of trade in WAPP are shown in Figure A1.3.

The total power exports arising from cross-border trade currently stand at approximately 3,500 gigawatt-hours, and there are currently four countries unable to benefit from regional trade due to lack of interconnectivity.

Transmission Pricing Methodology

The WAPP Transmission Pricing Methodology that is proposed for adoption in Phase 2 of the power trading arrangements is defined in an ERERA Resolution.[6]

---

[5] West African Power Pool. 2015. *2016–2019 Business Plan.* October. www.ecowapp.org.

[6] Resolution No. 006/ERERA/15. Adoption of the Tariff Methodology for Regional Transmission Cost and Tariff. http://icc.ecowapp.org/documents-resources; and https://erera.arrec.org/wp-content/uploads/2017/06/Transmission-Tariff-Methodology-August-2015-V4_signed.pdf.

Figure A1.3: Imports and Exports of the West African Power Pool, 2015

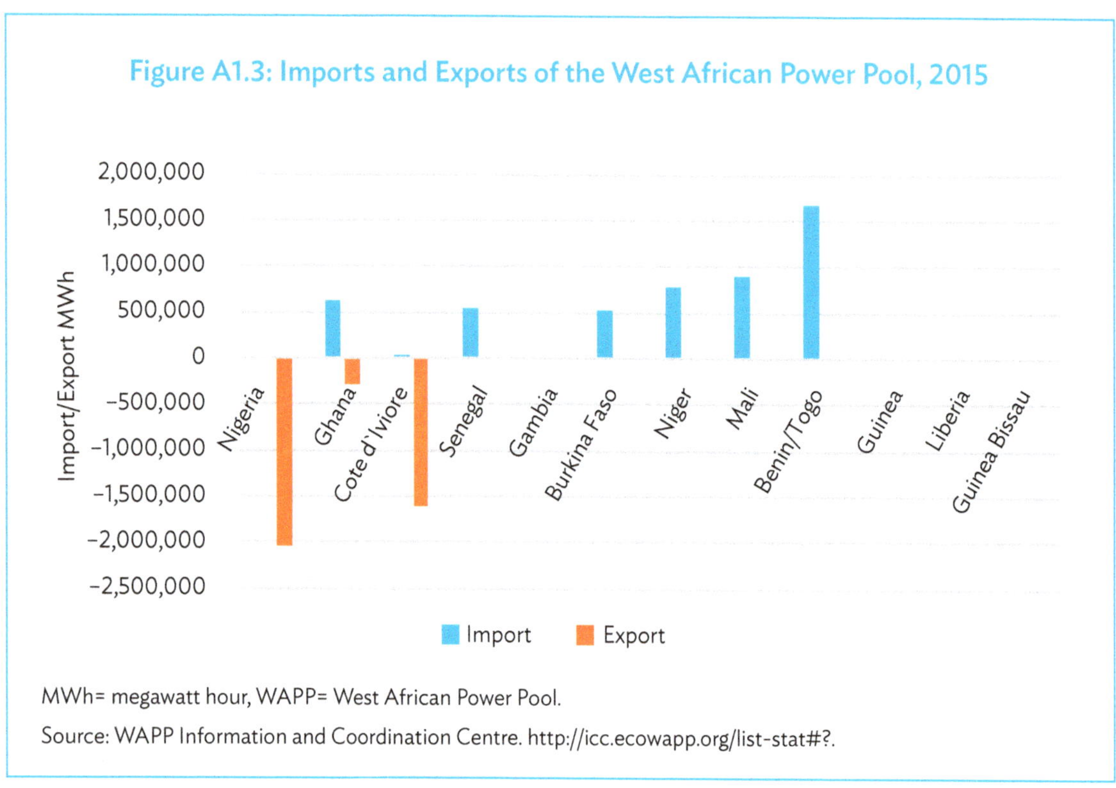

MWh= megawatt hour, WAPP= West African Power Pool.

Source: WAPP Information and Coordination Centre. http://icc.ecowapp.org/list-stat#?.

The key features of the proposed methodology are summarized below.

Overall approach and methodology

The Regional Transmission Tariff Methodology (RTTM) that has been selected for application in WAPP is a point-to-point MW-km flow-based method. It involves the calculation of a specific charge for each bilateral trade with wheeling power through a third-party network.

The key stages in the calculation include

- B.1 Determine the transmission assets used in the wheeling transaction in each national network, and the associated asset values.
- B.2 Calculate the annual revenue requirement for each national Transmission System Operator (TSO) transmission asset used in regional bilateral trading.
- B.3 Use a load-flow calculation to determine the actual use made of each transmission asset by each regional bilateral trade, and calculate the associated transmission losses.
- B.4 Calculate the total transmission revenue requirements for each TSO associated with regional bilateral trades.
- B.5 Calculate the transmission tariff and the transmission losses that are applicable to the power purchaser under each bilateral trade.

Definition of wheeling assets

The Regional Transmission Network is defined as all the transmission assets at voltages greater than 132 kilovolts (kV) in the ECOWAS power utilities' networks. In practice therefore, this means that all the 330 kV and 225 kV assets are included in the wheeling charge calculation. This definition could be revised by ERERA from time to time. The SMO is responsible for maintaining the asset database.

Asset values are to be calculated and then agreed by the WAPP Engineering and Operating Committee, based on a replacement valuation method.

Calculation of annual revenue requirements for transmission assets

Asset values are calculated as Depreciated Replacement Costs. The lifetimes adopted for the different asset types are as follows:

- transmission lines: 50 years
- substation equipment: 25 years
- substation civil works: 50 years
- transformers: 25 years

The option to be adopted exists in the RTTM for a single asset life of 30 years.

A formula is proposed for calculating the weighted average cost of capital (WACC), which is then used for determining the annuitized cost of each transmission asset that should be recoverable by the TSO that owns and operates the asset.

An allowance is added for O&M costs, which is applied as a margin on the capital cost of the asset at a rate between 2% and 5% of the capital cost per annum. The actual percentage to be used is determined by ERERA.

Calculation of transmission use of system and losses

The actual use of the transmission assets and the associated network losses are calculated using load flow study, which is based on the maximum generation hour across the regional network for the year ahead.

In the load flow study, the regional bilateral trade being investigated is removed, and the load flow is solved. The trade is then reinstated and those transmission elements identified on which the power flow increases by 1% or more. Similarly, the increase (or reduction) in system losses associated with the trade is calculated for each asset.

Calculation of Transmission System Operator revenue requirements

From the load flow results and the percentage utilization of each asset by the different bilateral trades, the total revenue requirement for each TSO arising from each regional trade can be determined. The sum of these defines the total revenue that should be allocated to the TSO arising from bilateral trades. In the event that an asset is built specifically to enable a single bilateral trade, the percentage of its use for trading will be set to 100%.

The cost of losses incurred on the TSO's system arising from each bilateral trade is determined using the load flow results and a tariff for losses that is determined by ERERA.

Calculation of charges for each bilateral trade
The transmission charges to be paid by the purchaser in each bilateral trade are calculated from the sum of the proportion of the TSOs' revenue requirements attributable to each trade. This is calculated using the percentage utilization of each asset and the asset value.

System and Market Operator responsibilities
The SMO will be responsible for applying the RTTM to calculate charges on an annual basis, and for collecting revenues from the purchasers of bilateral trades relating to transmission charges and losses. The SMO will then redistribute these to the relevant TSOs.

Detailed procedures are to be developed to enable the SMO to fulfill its obligations and to define the requirements for TSOs to submit data to ensure the accuracy of the models and calculations

Appendix 2: Examples of Regional Balancing Arrangements

A2.1 Introduction

One of the main means available to the Greater Mekong Subregion (GMS) in promoting an efficient electricity sector in the region is to develop a robust energy market for trading energy ahead of real time.

In order for a market to develop properly, a reliable methodology for settling imbalances in the system is required. This requirement has its basis in the need for an instantaneous balance between supply and demand in the power system to assure quality of supply. The energy market platforms ahead of real time will ensure that offers and bids are matched ahead of the real time operation of the system. Between a given point in time and the real time operation, the status of individual generators and/or the demand level might have changed, implying that the scheduling of other generators and/or loads will have to change in order to maintain the required balance. The imbalances (either caused by excess or reduced generation compared to the original schedules and/or consumption above or below the original schedules) need to be settled properly to have price certainty and to reduce price volatility in the market—both of these are factors are crucial to gaining confidence in the market itself.

The traditional system dealing with the imbalances is an "in-kind" arrangement whereby the differences between the net scheduled energy and the actual net exchanged energy (referred to as inadvertent energy) should be returned during a time period when they have approximately the same value as when they occur. This approach, while acceptable during the early stages of developing cross-border trading, is incompatible with the requirements of a modern and efficient market-based system, where imbalances are settled in cash. It nevertheless represents a reasonable starting point for the development of regional trading.

A2.2 International Balancing Markets and Mechanisms

This section summarizes the balancing markets and mechanisms in other interconnections, specifically in Europe, the Nordic region, the United States (US), and the Southern African Power Pool (SAPP). The key areas examined are balancing principles and providers, balance and imbalance volume calculations, and pricing of balancing and imbalances. The interconnections have all developed different approaches which are based on history, power plant make up, political environment, and economics.

Balancing Principles and Providers

The initial phase of developing a balancing market and/or mechanism is identifying the principles for balancing and the possible providers of balancing services.

Balancing is the energy provided over and above the day ahead and intraday scheduled energy in the second to minutes balancing of frequency of the interconnection. The interconnection can be broken into sections such as individual countries and technical boundaries where congestion occurs. The sections can be separately responsible for their own balancing, called control areas which can be a transmission system operator (TSO) or a group of TSOs.

Power plants that are flexible can respond to frequency changes from 5 seconds to 30 minutes, depending on the technology and design.

The variations in balancing principles for each interconnection have their foundations in the same core principles.

Continental Europe

Continental Europe has historically had at least one control area for each country. Germany had a control area for each state within the country (similar to the US). Each control area was responsible for balancing itself. Area control error (ACE) calculations are used to calculate the megawatt (MW) shortfall or surplus within the control area.

The time frames for frequency control (balancing) are broken into three categories:

- **Fast-acting reserve** at each flexible power plant to prevent the frequency from deviating too much, known as primary frequency control and recently renamed as frequency containment reserve (FCR). Primary frequency control was the responsibility of all power plants but has been reduced to only a few power plants. The speed of response is full activation in 30 seconds, which is based on the loss of a 3,000 MW nuclear power station in the interconnection with a minimum frequency of 49.2 hertz (Hz).
- **Secondary frequency control reserve** which can quickly restore the frequency in the defaulting control area (starting within 15 seconds to match the primary response). The fast start of restoration leads to the requirement of the control area automating secondary frequency control; the algorithm is known as automatic generation control (AGC). The control area is required to restore itself within 15 minutes; the frequency variation is Europe is small, and there is very little risk to restore over such a long time period. Secondary frequency control reserve has been renamed as frequency restoration reserve (FRR). FRR is broken into two categories: aFRR, which is automatically activated (using AGC or something similar) and mFRR which is manually activated (using telephone).
- **Tertiary frequency control reserve** is required to restore secondary frequency control for large changes in generation (a unit trip) or demand changes (loss of a large consumer). Tertiary frequency control reserve has been renamed as restoration reserve.

In recent developments, the move has been toward reserve sharing and combining control areas into large areas by using "virtual tie lines." Germany is now combined into a single control area for secondary frequency control. Spain and Portugal; Slovenia, Croatia, Bosnia, and Herzegovina; and Serbia,

Montenegro, and Macedonia are all common blocks (control areas). Belgium and the Netherlands are pre-netting to reduce the amount of cross border activations. Pre-netting involves adding two ACEs, which results in an overall ACE less than or equal to the sum of the two. All of these arrangements are to reduce overall reserve activations resulting in lower balancing and imbalance charges.

Nordic Region

The Nordic region operates as a single interconnection (control area) and there is no tie-line control between countries.

The reserves for frequency control are defined as the same with Europe, except for secondary frequency control, wherein the full activation time is within two minutes. Automatic secondary frequency control is shared between countries according to peak demand, and reserve is activated proportionally to all automatic participants in the Nordic region. The predominant reason for this is the large number of available hydropower plants in the Nordic region, which can respond in two minutes.

There is a centralized dispatch for activation of manually activated secondary and tertiary reserves, which is achieved from a common merit order for the region taking into account congestion.

US–North American Electricity Reliability Corporation

The US used to have numerous control areas, at least one per state; but these have been combined under independent system operators (ISOs) to create larger control areas covering more than one state, including Pennsylvania–New Jersey–Maryland (PJM), New York ISO, New England ISO, and California ISO. The North American Electric Reliability Council (NERC) in the US has refined the provision of reserves for balancing, and requires all control areas to balance themselves, becoming known as balancing authorities.

Balancing services are provided through the Regulation Reserve, which must balance the system minute to minute. The frequency bias for the ACE calculation is based on the calculation of Interconnection Frequency Response for the interconnection.

For a multiple Balancing Authority interconnection, the interconnection frequency response obligation (FRO) is allocated based on the balancing authority's annual load and annual generation.

The FRO allocation is based on the following formula:

FROBA = IFRO × (Annual GenBA + Annual LoadBA)/(Annual GenInt + Annual LoadInt)

where
- IFRO is the total Interconnection Frequency Response Obligation
- FROBA is the Frequency Response Obligation for a particular Balancing Authority
- Annual GenBA is the total annual "Output of Generating Plants" within the balancing authority area (BAA)
- Annual LoadBA is the total annual Load within the BAA
- Annual GenInt is the sum of all Annual GenBA values reported in that interconnection
- Annual LoadInt is the sum of all Annual LoadBA values reported in that interconnection

There is a requirement for the operating reserve to cover for the greater of the largest single contingency, or 3% of hourly load plus 3% hourly generation. A total of 50% of operating reserve must be spinning and the rest can be non-spinning, known as supplemental reserve. Spinning reserve must be synchronized on governing and should be available in 10 minutes. Supplemental reserve is any generation or demand side option that can respond in 10 minutes.

Southern African Power Pool

The SAPP has three control areas:

- South Africa control area (includes Swaziland, Lesotho, Botswana, Namibia, and Southern Mozambique),
- Zimbabwe control area, and
- Zambia control area (which includes the southern part of the DRC and Copper Energy Belt Company).

In SAPP, the operating reserve requirement is defined as 1.5 times the largest generating unit, which is 920 MW. Operating reserve for 2017 is 1,420 MW. Half of this total reserve must consist of the automatically activated spinning reserve (FCR) and should be fully active in 10 seconds. Each TSO carries a portion of this reserve using an 'old' NERC formula

$$\mathbf{SORR = PORR \times (2Ds/Dt + Us/Ut) / 3}$$

where,

SORR = minimum system operating reserve requirement,

PORR = total pool operating reserve requirement,

Ds = individual system's annual peak demand,

Dt = total sum of individual system's annual peak demand, and

Us = individual system's largest unit. (sum of Us)

South Africa's TSO, Eskom, provides these reserves on behalf of all members in its control area, which are Botswana, Mozambique, Swaziland, Lesotho, and Namibia.

Eskom also undertakes dynamic studies to calculate automatic FCR requirements for the loss of largest credible multiple contingency (920 MW - 2040 MW) to ensure frequency remains above 49.0 Hz for these contingencies. Historically, these incidents occur at least four times a year.

The three control areas in Zambia, Zimbabwe, and South Africa are responsible for balancing, and are required to have AGC installed to ensure ACE is controlled. Control areas must be within 25 MWh of day-ahead schedule for each hour of the day. Day-ahead schedule can be adjusted with intraday trades.

Gulf Cooperation Council

In the Gulf States, the Gulf Cooperation Centre Interchange Authority (GCCIA) rules require a sharing of primary and secondary reserves based on the United Kingdom's definitions for primary frequency control—wherein primary reserve is fully available in 5 seconds and sustainable for a further 25 seconds, and secondary reserve is fully active in 25 seconds and sustainable for a further 30 minutes. Both primary and secondary reserves are activated by frequency deviation and thus, do not consider interchanges between countries.

Total primary reserve is the largest contingency in the GCC interconnection plus 10%. Largest unit is 660 MW and primary reserve is 726 MW. Each TSO must contribute to the correction of a disturbance in accordance with its respective contribution coefficient to primary reserve (ENTSO-E allocation methodology). This contribution coefficient (Ci) is calculated on a regular basis for the TSO's system, using the following formula

$$Ci=Gi/Gu$$

whereas

Gi = the total online active generation in the TSO transmission system "i "(including electricity production for export); and

Gu = the total (sum of) online system active generation in all the TSO transmission systems of the combined system, including the 60 Hz side East TSO.

The back-to-back 50/60 Hz HVDC system is programmed to provide primary reserve and secondary reserve during disturbances in either of the 50 Hz or 60 Hz interconnection.

Control areas are not defined per se but individual countries within the GCC area must balance themselves and be within 50 MWh of the day-ahead schedule for each hour of the day.

GMS Proposal for Balancing Service Principles and Providers in the Long Term

Balancing is the function of matching supply and demand in real time. The proposed GMS market design is such that participants and TSOs can bilaterally trade power up to one hour before real time. The net position of all contracts is the binding contract between participants, participants and TSO, and between TSOs. Between this time and real time, there could be a change in the status of individual generators and/or in-demand levels. TSOs and participants will have to change the reported schedules with generators and/or loads to ensure that the balance between supply and demand is maintained in real time, given the changes that have taken place.

The formation of control areas can be the current GMS countries but is not limited to this. TSOs can be combined and form a common control area or even form a single control area for the GMS. Reserve sharing between control areas should be allowed.

Control areas use automatic generation control (AGC) and manual instructions to non-AGC units to maintain the balance between supply and demand in their control area. The correct schedules would have to be registered in the control system to calculate the correct ACE.

Balance and Imbalance Volume Calculations

Imbalance energy can be defined as the difference between actual metered energy and scheduled energy. However, this can be more complicated as energy flows due to mutual support through primary frequency support or through other support requested within the scheduled period. The support provided is called balancing energy as it is used to maintain balance. If the price of the energy sold and bought is the same, identifying then whether the energy is balancing energy or imbalance energy does not matter.

Many interconnections also recognize that it is difficult to control the power exactly on schedule and have thus created a term called "inadvertent energy." This energy is typically paid back in kind on a same-time-same-day principle, otherwise the inadvertent energy is not compensated or reconciled.

Continental Europe

Continental Europe control areas used inadvertent energy to reconcile imbalance energy as the energy flows were insignificant when compared to the bilateral agreements. With the recent market developments and increase in renewable wind and solar generation, inadvertent energy is calculated every 15 minutes between control areas. Inadvertent energy is calculated as the difference between actual and scheduled power flows. There are a few markets that are operational, so the schedule is from the "gate closure" (from the last market that operated in the region).

According to the Electricity Balancing Guidelines, all TSOs performing the automatic frequency restoration process, pursuant to Part IV of Commission Regulation (EU) 2017/1485, shall use the European process to operate the imbalance netting process.[7] TSOs have started Imbalance Netting Cooperation (INC) with focus on the pilot projects: International Grid Control Cooperation (IGCC), e-GCC, and the INC. To commence the implementation of this European process, TSOs have agreed to use the IGCC as a reference project and thereby as a starting point. The process is shown graphically in Figure A2.1.

The IGCC is a regional project operating the imbalance netting process, which currently involves 11 TSOs from 8 countries. These are the TSOs from Austria (APG), Belgium (Elia), Switzerland (Swissgrid), Czech Republic (CEPS), Germany (50Hertz, Amprion, TenneT DE, TransnetBW), Denmark (Energinet.dk), France (RTE), and the Netherlands (TenneT NL).

IGCC is currently operational in Germany only, and uses the available cross-border capacities after every energy market gate closure and the ACEs of the different TSOs. The IGCC provides a correction signal modifying the ACE in each of the involved secondary controllers, thus preventing an overcompensation of the ACE or activations that can increase the overall system imbalance instead of limiting it at a regional scale.

The Grid Control Cooperation is based on an automatic Frequency Restoration Reserves (aFRR)-Optimization System for the activation of aFRR.

Imbalance netting in the context of IGCC is the process agreed between TSOs of two or more load frequency control (LFC) areas within one or more than one synchronous area. Such process prevents simultaneous aFRR activation in opposite directions by taking into account the respective area control errors and the activated aFRR and correcting the input of the involved frequency restoration processes accordingly.

The imbalance energy between TSOs in Germany (IGCC participating TSOs in the future) is in essence not controlled, but the goal is to reduce the overall imbalance energy in the region as long as there are no congestion problems within IGCC. Imbalance energy accounts for 3% of the total energy, and the netting positive and negative imbalances that occur at the same time significantly reduce total system imbalances.

[7] European Commission. 2017. COMMISSION REGULATION (EU) 2017/2195 of 23 November 2017 establishing a guideline on electricity balancing. https://eur-lex.europa.eu/legal-content/EN/TXT/?uri=uriserv:OJ.L_.2017.312.01.0006.01.ENG&toc=OJ:L:2017:312:TOC#d1e1650-6-1.

Figure A2.1: Example of Imbalance Netting

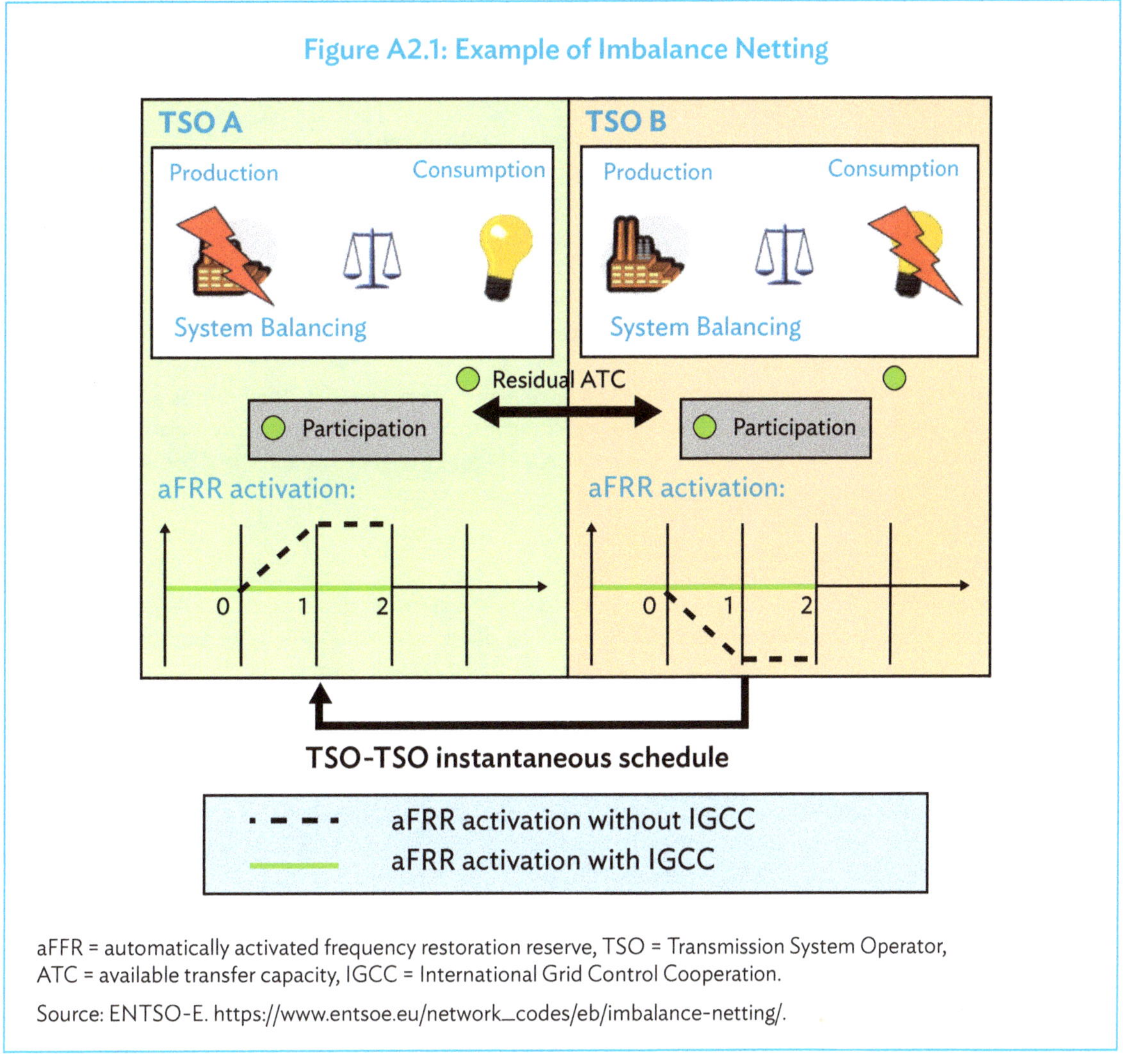

aFFR = automatically activated frequency restoration reserve, TSO = Transmission System Operator, ATC = available transfer capacity, IGCC = International Grid Control Cooperation.

Source: ENTSO-E. https://www.entsoe.eu/network_codes/eb/imbalance-netting/.

Nordic Region

The Nordic region's interconnection calculates imbalance energy as the difference between actual power flows and day-ahead scheduled energy flows. This is calculated by the hour, but the goal is to reduce the period to 15 minutes as per EU rules and guidelines.

US–North American Electric Reliability Corporation

Inadvertent energy is calculated as the difference between actual and scheduled power flows for each balancing authority. There are only a few markets operational, so the schedule is from the "gate closure" (from the last market that operated in the region). NERC allows dynamic schedules between Balancing Authorities; these schedules can change as fast as every two seconds, so the imbalance energy can be the net position after the dynamic schedule.

California Independent System Operator (CAISO) calculates imbalance energy as follows:

For generator: imbalance energy = metered energy – scheduled energy

For load: imbalance energy = scheduled energy – metered energy

There is a further level of refinement where the energy is calculated as instructed balance energy and uninstructed imbalance energy. Instructions are issued every 5 minutes but settled on 10-minute intervals. Uninstructed imbalance energy is subject to a penalty if it deviates beyond tolerance band (the greater of 3% of the maximum power, Pmax, or 5 MW). Units on AGC (Regulation Reserve) have their compliance with instructions measured and separately accounted for.

New England ISO, PJM ISO, and New York ISO all have 5-minute market trading periods and all energy is settled on actual metered values. The TSO does not take into account bilateral agreements between two or more parties and there is no physical settlement process for energy provided or not provided under these bilateral agreements.

Southern African Power Pool

The SAPP interconnection calculates imbalance energy as the difference between actual power flows and day-ahead plus bilateral scheduled energy flows. The day ahead schedules can be adjusted by intra-day trading. If imbalance energy is less than 25 MWh between control areas, then this treated as inadvertent energy.

Gulf Cooperation Council

GCCIA calculates imbalance energy as the difference between actual power flows and scheduled bilateral energy flows. The day-ahead schedules can be adjusted by intra-day bilateral trading. If imbalance energy is less than 50 MWh between control areas, then this is treated as inadvertent energy, and the bilateral trade schedule is adjusted for the same time on the next similar day.

Proposed Balance and Imbalance Volume Calculations for the GMS

The balance and imbalance volume between control areas is the hourly difference between actual power flow and scheduled power flow. The balance and imbalance volumes within a control area between TSOs, and between TSOs and individual GMS participants, should use the same methodology for consistency; however, TSOs and individual participants can have hedging arrangements to mitigate price exposure.

Pricing of Balancing and Imbalances

The provision of balancing services is voluntary but exposure to imbalance energy prices is not and depends on whether a participant is in balance or not.

There can be a single price for all imbalances resulting from balancing actions and imbalances. The imbalance price can be determined from the weighted average price per costs paid to balancing service providers, or the marginal price per cost of the most expensive service provider.

The price or cost from a balancing service provider is either the bid price (market price) or a predetermined cost for the type of generation providing the balancing (mechanism price).

Imbalance energy prices can be determined for the energy sold and purchased by the providers of balance energy and for the sources of imbalance energy. Both are to sell and buy imbalance energy, such that there is a buy price and a separate sell price for each settlement period.

Continental Europe

Imbalance pricing is the most complicated technical and commercial issue that is regulated in the Continental European electricity sector. The imbalance pricing for each TSO is calculated on the basis of the opportunity price (avoided cost) that each TSO has gained from importing or exporting balancing energy instead of activating more expensive local reserve. Prices are to be determined every 15 minutes.

The underlying principle is to share netting benefits in a fair manner among members, reflecting the "opportunity value" of the avoided balancing charges.

Nordic Region

The Nordic region's interconnection calculates imbalance prices based on the weighted average of activated manual Frequency Response Reserve (mFRR) in the region when there is no congestion. If there is congestion toward a zone, then there is a separate price calculated for the congested zone. This is based on the zonal activated mFRR weighted average price. The price in the congested zone is higher than that of the rest of the uncongested system. Imbalance energy between two zones with different prices is calculated at the average price between the two zones.

Imbalance energy resulting from the activation of primary frequency control (FCR) and automatic secondary control (aFRR) is priced at the same imbalance price that was calculated for mFRR. These service providers are thus price takers.

US-North American Electric Reliability Corporation

The California Independent System Operator (CAISO) calculates imbalance prices for instructed balances and uninstructed imbalances as follows:

- regulation energy (units on AGC) paid as instructed energy at zonal market clearing price (MCP);
- balancing resources paid at 10-minute resource specific price (10-minute bid price);
- imbalance participants where deviation is less than 5% or 5 MW imbalance price is the zonal ex-post price; and
- imbalance participants where deviation is greater than 5% or 5 MW imbalance price is the resource specific price (participants' bid price).

New England ISO, PJM ISO, and New York ISO all have 5-minute market trading periods and all energy is priced at the post-dispatch locational marginal price (LMP).

Southern African Power Pool

Initially the SAPP resolved the inadvertent energy through in-kind settlement, but this soon became impractical due to same countries constantly taking inadvertent energy and not returning it on the prescribed time.

SAPP thus resolved to implement a cash settlement method and introduced a frequency-based imbalance energy rates calculation based on day-ahead market (DAM) clearing prices. The frequency-based imbalance formula was initially developed in India and has been used for real time balancing prices for many years.

The energy imbalance price when the frequency is between 49.95 Hz and 50.05 Hz is the day-ahead market clearing price for the hour. The structure of imbalance energy rates is shown in Figure A2.2.

The imbalance energy price then linearly increases if the average frequency is below 49.95 Hz to a maximum energy imbalance price of twice the DAM clearing price for that hour, if average frequency for the interconnection is below 49.85 Hz. Conversely if the average frequency is above 50.05 Hz, the payment is half the day-ahead clearing price for the hour, and decreasing to no payment for imbalances if hourly frequency average is above the normal frequency range of 50.15 Hz (this is common as Eskom's coal-fired power plants cannot operate below 60% capacity, and it is very expensive to take them off the system every evening).

Figure A2.2: SAPP Hourly Hertz-Based Methodology for Imbalance Energy Rates

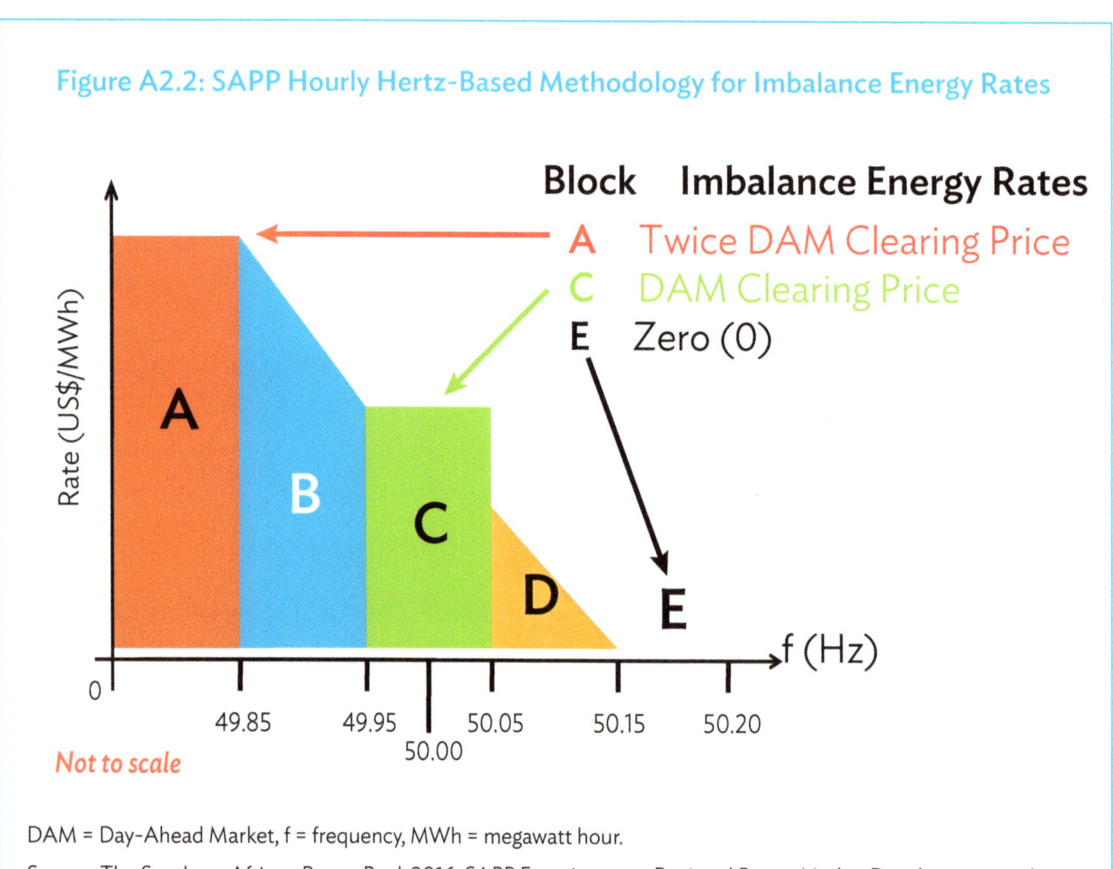

DAM = Day-Ahead Market, f = frequency, MWh = megawatt hour.

Source: The Southern African Power Pool. 2016. SAPP Experience on Regional Power Market Development and Operation. Presentation to South Asian Region. New Delhi, India. 15 January. https://sari-energy.org/wp-content/uploads/2016/03/Session-3-Mr-Musara-BETA-SAPP.pdf.

Gulf Cooperation Council
The Gulf Cooperation Centre Interchange Authority (GCCIA) has inadvertent energy rules in place: if imbalance energy is less than 50 MWh between control areas, then the bilateral schedule for the same time on the next similar day is adjusted. If the imbalance energy is above 50 MWh, then the imbalance energy is priced at open-cycle gas turbine prices.

Proposed Pricing of Balancing and Imbalances for the GMS
The pricing of balancing services and imbalances requires knowing the prices of activations in balancing in the GMS. From the research described earlier, Continental Europe, the Nordic market, and the US use the bids and offers from balancing participants. Southern Africa uses the day-ahead market clearing price as a reference and Gulf States use open-cycle gas turbines as the typical marginal unit.

The GMS does not have bids and offers from balancing participants or day-ahead market clearing price to reference. The price for balancing services could use reference prices in the short-term bilateral market, but these prices are not meant to be disclosed to all participants; and it is not guaranteed that there will always be short-term bilateral trades for each hour of the day.

Figure A2.3: Marginal Unit Stack Formation Framework

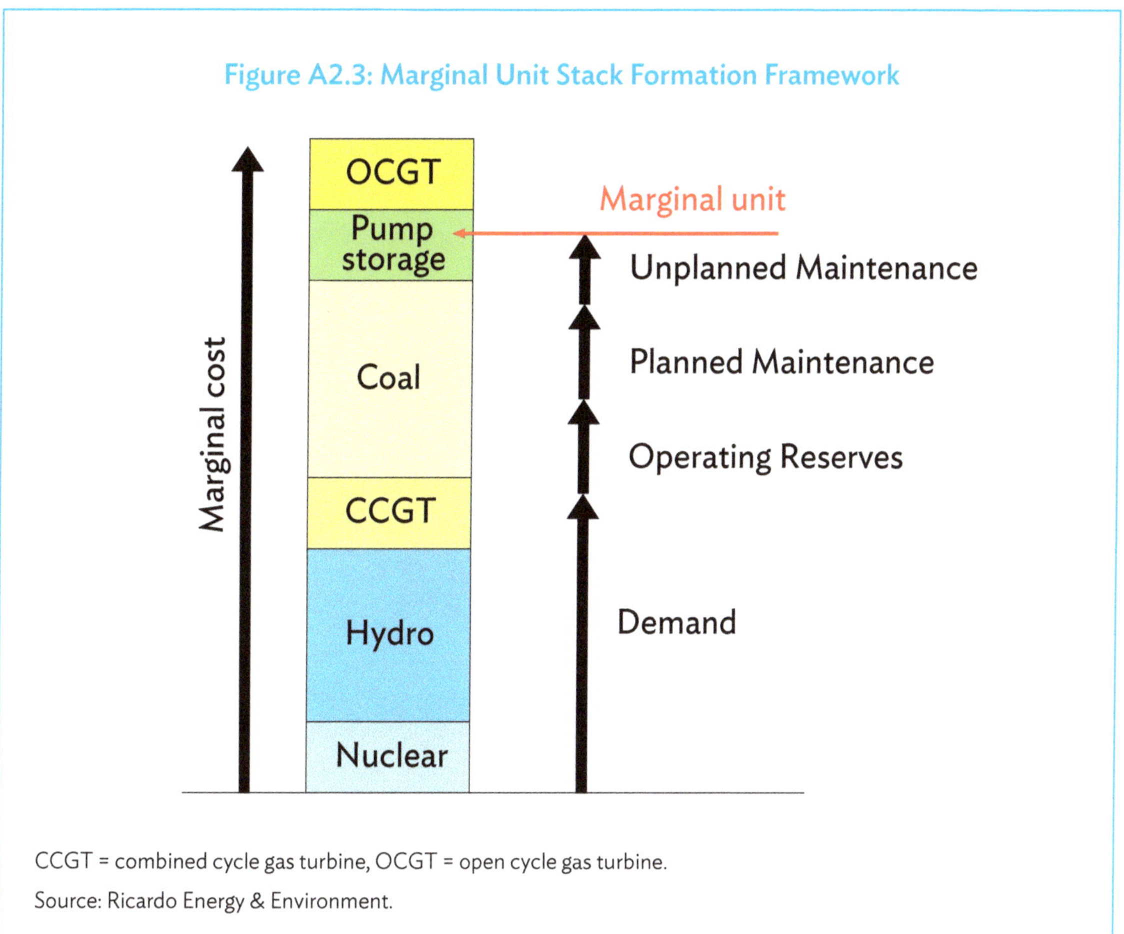

CCGT = combined cycle gas turbine, OCGT = open cycle gas turbine.

Source: Ricardo Energy & Environment.

The proposed alternative is to have a reference price based on the marginal unit type on the system. The reference price is the typical price for the unit type whether this be hydro, combined-cycle gas, coal power station or open-cycle gas turbine. Many institutions publish these prices.

The marginal unit stack is fixed for the year (or season) and the demand for the balancing hour is known. The marginal unit is determined by adding operating reserves to the demand, planned maintenance (which could be a percentage or actual maintenance) and unplanned maintenance (which is typically a percentage). All participants know the reference price and can choose to obtain balancing services from the predetermined stack or to self-provide from their own internal balancing service providers.

All balances and imbalances can thus be settled at the reference price. The proposal is not to have a dead-band for inadvertent energy, as the dead band is difficult to determine (and is for parties to agree upon).

A further premium could be added to the reference price using a similar sliding scale developed by India/SAPP with a reference to average frequency. The second option is to use the NERC "ACE based" performance to add a premium onto the reference price. The operating guidelines already refer to NERC Control Performance Standard 1 (CPS1), Control Performance Standard 2 (CPS2), and Disturbance Control Standard 1 (DCS1). NERC has replaced CPS2 with the Balancing Authority ACE Limit (BAAL) but the principles of measuring average ACE still remain.

Where there is congestion, then two stacks are required, and the congested region has an equal or higher price. Cheap resources from the uncongested region cannot be used for balancing the congested region due to transmission constraints. The imbalance energy flowing across the transmission congestion is exposed to the price difference between two market areas. The proposal is, the price of imbalance energy is at the average of the two prices. There is thus no income surplus (or shortfall), and the benefits are shared between the two TSOs as is done in Continental Europe.

Appendix 3: The Lao PDR–Thailand–Malaysia–Singapore Power Integration Project

Overview

The proposal for this power trade project was first put forward during the special Senior Official Meeting on Energy (SOME) in December 2013. During subsequent meetings of the Association of Southeast Asian Nations (ASEAN), the proposal was welcomed and discussed by electricity sector stakeholders from each of the countries involved.

The trade project is technically viable; the power could be transmitted from Lao PDR to Thailand through existing interconnections (115 kV).[8] The power could also be transmitted between Thailand and Malaysia through the KNE-Gurun 300 kV 300 MW HVDC line. The power flows on this high voltage direct current (HVDC) line could be controlled through the HVDC control mechanism. The existing 275 kV between Plentong and Senoko could be used to transfer power between Malaysia and Singapore.

Figure A3.1 illustrates the interconnectors between various countries.

The commercial arrangements that were originally proposed for the project as a whole were developed, as shown in Figure A3.2. This included a structure of wheeling charge agreements (WCAs) covering the payments due to the Electricity Generating Authority of Thailand (EGAT) and Tenga Nasional Berhad (TNB) for the use of their transmission networks for wheeling power from the Lao PDR to Singapore, and a power purchase agreement (PPA) between Electricite de Laos (EDL) and Singapore Power for the power purchase.

The first phase of the LTMS-PIP project involves the signing of a combined energy purchase and wheeling agreement (EPWA) covering the purchase of 100 MW by TNB in Malaysia from Electrite du Cambodge (EDC) in the Lao PDR, and the wheeling of power through the EGAT transmission network in Thailand. The EPWA was signed on 27 September 2017 during the ASEAN Ministers on Energy Meeting (AMEM) held in the Philippines. The EPWA contains provisions to deal with the following key aspects of the LTMS-PIP trade, including

- energy payments from TNB to EDL;
- wheeling charge payments from EDL to EGAT (note that these are payments made by the energy seller to the wheeling service provider only);

[8] International Energy Cooperation Office, Ministry of Energy, Government of Thailand. Lao PDR – Thailand – Malaysia – Singapore Power Trade Project. http://www.energyforum2015.com/download/Session1-3present.pdf.

Figure A3.1: Lao PDR–Thailand–Malaysia–Singapore Power Trade Project

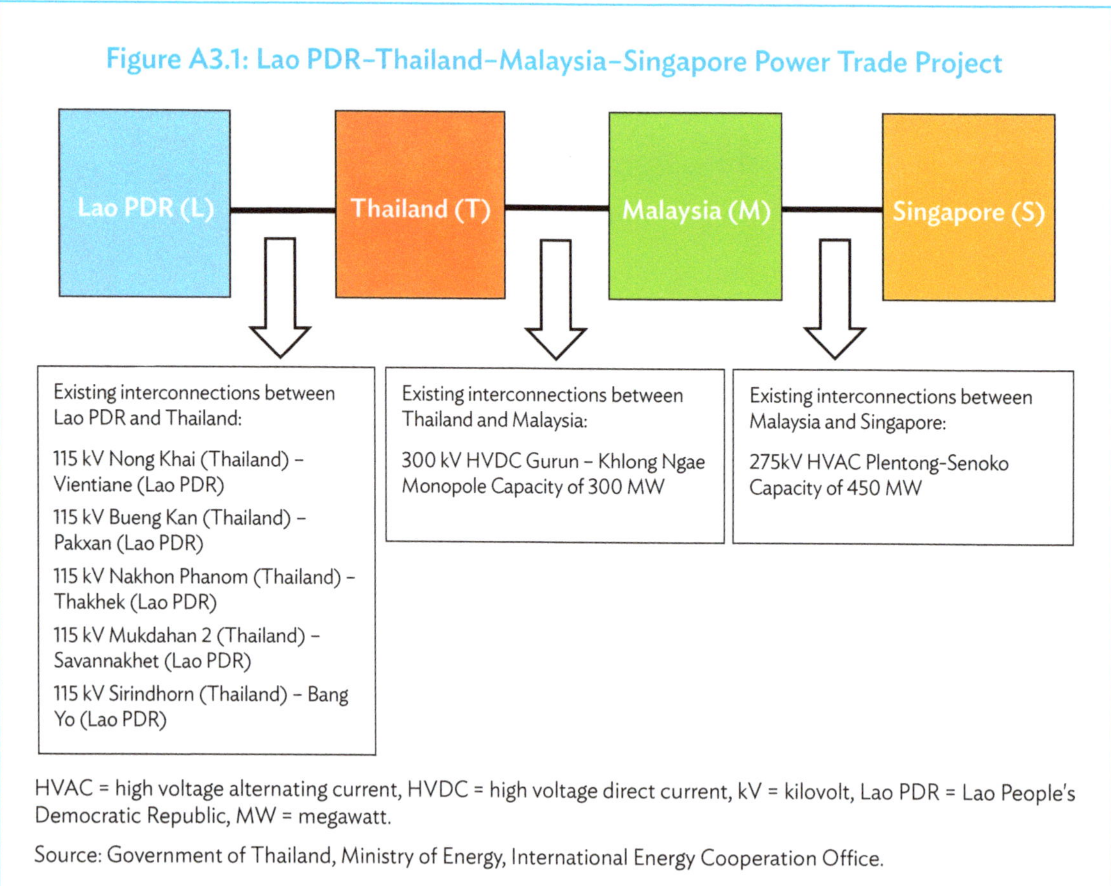

HVAC = high voltage alternating current, HVDC = high voltage direct current, kV = kilovolt, Lao PDR = Lao People's Democratic Republic, MW = megawatt.

Source: Government of Thailand, Ministry of Energy, International Energy Cooperation Office.

- the delivery by EDL of energy to EGAT to compensate for the losses incurred on the EGAT system due to the wheeling transaction;
- arrangements for EGAT to cover any shortfall in the energy supplied by EDL to TNB, subject to a cap on the accumulated energy deficit that can arise before EGAT suspends its obligation to provide wheeling services. The EDL has to restore the energy deficit via energy transfers, or by cash payments, from EDL to EGAT before wheeling services will be reinstated; and
- situations where the transmission grid in the TNB or EGAT systems is constrained in its ability to accept or wheel power in accordance with the EPWA.

The second phase of the project would extend to trading with Singapore; however, Singapore currently has transparent competitive bidding for its supplies internally and decisions will be required as to how international trade could be introduced in the domestic market. One option for Singapore could be to give a direct contract to the international trade and bypass the normal competitive market processes. The electricity markets of the Lao PDR, Thailand, and Malaysia, being dominated by vertically integrated utilities, are such that the international trade envisaged by this interconnection project could be carried out by signing a simple power purchase agreement (PPA). Separate wheeling charge agreements (WCAs) are proposed for the use of the Thailand's and Malaysia's transmission networks, which would be entered into by Singapore as the purchasing entity.

Figure A3.2: Proposed Commercial Arrangements

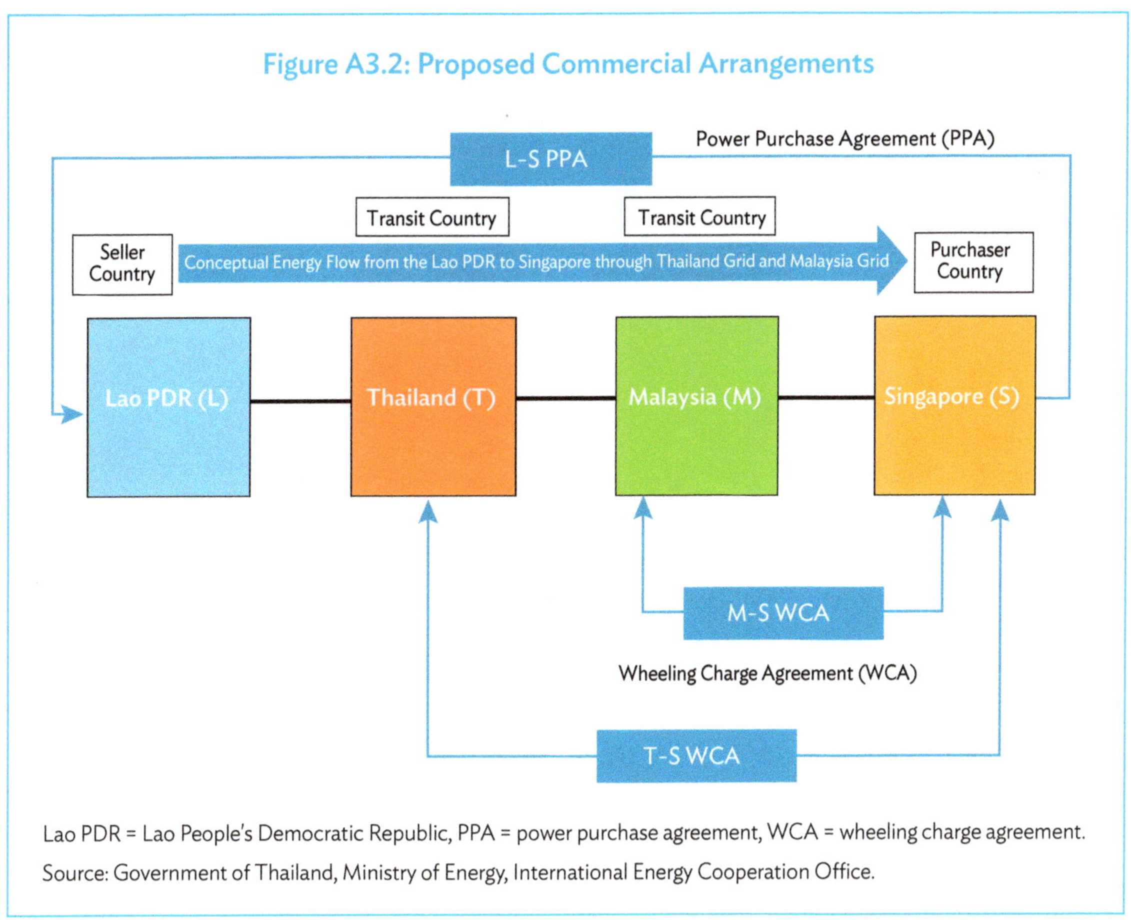

Lao PDR = Lao People's Democratic Republic, PPA = power purchase agreement, WCA = wheeling charge agreement.

Source: Government of Thailand, Ministry of Energy, International Energy Cooperation Office.

The situation that Singapore faces in this project is exactly analogous to that which Viet Nam will encounter once the Vietnamese Wholesale Electricity Market (VWEM) becomes active, and further consideration is therefore needed as to how international trade will be integrated into the operation of the domestic market.

Key Learning from the LTMS-PIP Project

The first phase of the LTMS-PIP project is an important example to consider in relation to the expansion of power trading in the GMS, because it is representative of the type of trading that is envisaged in the Stage 2 model defined in MoU-2 and the "Scenario 2" trading defined in Chapter 1. The key elements of the project which have potential application elsewhere are the following:

- Integration of commercial arrangements for power sales and wheeling into a tripartite agreement involving the buyer, the seller, and the wheeling service provider. For the short-term development of power trading in the GMS, bilateral contracts that can be entered into readily will be essential and having contractual structures and examples that make this possible will be highly beneficial. Phase 1 of the LTMS-PIP project provides a useful precedent for further consideration by GMS countries.

- Definition of wheeling within the EPWA is wide enough to cover the recovery of all the key costs to which EGAT, as the wheeling utility, is exposed. This includes
  (i) a MW-mile approach to the recovery of the costs of transmission assets;
  (ii) losses charges based on simulation of the import and export of the proposed 100 MW power transfer and taking account of the system marginal price in Thailand;
  (iii) balancing charges to make good of any shortfall in the energy delivered from Laos into Thailand and exported from Thailand into Malaysia (either in-kind or via cash settlement); and
  (iv) the recovery of an appropriate level of administration charges.[9]

[9] Future Cross-Border Trade and the ASEAN Power Grid. http://www.appp.or.th/imgadmins/document/09105940.pdf.

Appendix 4: Detailed Methodology for Wheeling Charges

Wheeling Tariff Methodology Steps

This chapter provides the detailed methodology to determine the wheeling tariff for all bilateral trades.

Step 1: Determine regional transmission assets and asset value

The Regional Transmission Network should be defined as straightforward as possible; and all the network assets that could in principle be used for wheeling power across a national network should be included in the methodology.

A voltage-based definition is likely to be the easiest to apply, and it is suggested that all **interconnected** assets operating at voltages greater than or equal to 110 kV, or as otherwise agreed by the Regional Power Trade Coordination Committee (RPTCC) in the Greater Mekong Subregion (GMS) should be considered as potential wheeling assets.

The interconnected assets in each transmission system operator (TSO) should include all transmission elements at the specified voltage level, whether the elements are used for regional trading or not. This is because whether any one particular asset is used for power wheeling in practice will depend solely on the power flows that arise on the system as a result of individual trades.

The asset database will contain all assets defined by class and by TSO. Physical data for each network branch should be recorded, including

- line length,
- numbers of circuits,
- conductor type,
- tower types,
- voltage level,
- switchgear type and voltage, and
- transformer rating and voltage.

The commercial operating date of each asset should also be provided by the TSO.

The regional transmission asset database should be maintained by the Regional Power Coordination Centre (RPCC), or an equivalent body, and initially by the RPTCC. The database should be updated annually from the information provided by each TSO.

For each element in the regional transmission asset database, a replacement value should be agreed upon by the RPCC (or an appropriate subcommittee appointed for the purpose). The replacement values should be updated every five years (or more frequently, if agreed by the RPCC).

It is recommended that reference is made to the ADB study *Facilitating Regional Power Trading and Environmentally Sustainable Development of Electricity Infrastructure in the Greater Mekong Subregion*, in which data was collated regarding the different levels of transmission cost incurred in each GMS country.[10] This data should be updated using information from recent transmission projects where possible.

Step 2: Calculate annual revenue requirements for each TSO asset used for the regional bilateral trading

The cost components to be recovered are:

- capital costs of network plant and equipment, and
- operation and maintenance costs.

Calculation of asset value

The method for calculating annual asset value is the Depreciated Replacement Cost. This method recognizes that the replacement of specific parts of the transmission line (transformer, switchgear) will be at current asset value.

Typical lifetimes used for asset valuation are:

- transmission lines, 50 years;
- substation equipment, 25 years;
- substation civil works, 50 years; and
- transformers, 25 years.

For simplicity, a single asset value of 30 years could be chosen, or a set of lifetimes could be agreed through discussion between GMS countries.

It is important to note that the assets included in the wheeling asset database should take into account all the transmission equipment in the network, including:

- transmission lines;
- cables;
- switchgear (including circuit breakers, disconnectors, and protection equipment);

[10] ADB. 2010. *Facilitating Regional Power Trading and Environmentally Sustainable Development of Electricity Infrastructure in the Greater Mekong Subregion*. Manila. https://www.adb.org/projects/41018-012/main.

- transformers; and
- other ancillary equipment, such as compensation equipment installed on the network that is not covered by ancillary services payments.

Equipment costs should be stated as installed costs including civil works.

The total annuitized revenue requirement for each transmission asset made available for wheeling by the TSO is calculated as

TSO revenue requirement f or asset (i) = RAB(i) * WACC + D(i) + O&M(i)

where

RAB(i) = regulatory asset base = average of asset i's depreciated value before and after depreciation in a given year;

WACC = post-tax nominal weighted average capital cost;

D = depreciation in year y (Consideration could be given to depreciating assets to a minimum of half their original value as a means of giving adequate financial incentives for TSOs to continue providing wheeling services in the future.); and

O&M = operation and maintenance costs in a year, typically calculated as a percentage of the original capital cost of the line, plus an allowance for the relevant administration and management costs of the TSO associated with providing the wheeling services.

Calculation of WACC

WACC is used in the wheeling charge calculation as part of the process of calculating an annuitized cost for each transmission asset forming part of the regional transmission asset base.

The WACC values allowed will be agreed by the RPCC. Ideally all countries should use the same WACC values for regional interconnector asset value calculation, to maximize the transparency of the methodology; however, the ability to agree on a common WACC for all countries in the GMS will depend on factors such as the differences in the risks of investing in individual countries and foreign exchange risk.

For dedicated interconnectors constructed through special purpose entities (SPEs) or other private-owned transmission assets, the WACC values could be actual WACC values in the agreement. This could apply in the case of a private developer of transmission constructing specific interconnection assets that are to be used for wheeling.

Taxation on international transmission company profits. The formula for WACC allows for company taxation of the transmission companies' profits. Each transmission company will be registered in one particular country and the taxation will apply to that country only.

Intergovernmental agreements will have to be reached to harmonize taxation policies on transmission businesses if a standardized approach to taxation is required.

Operation and maintenance costs. It is recommended that operation and maintenance costs are recovered by applying a predetermined margin to the capital costs of equipment to cover the annual O&M costs of the lines and associated equipment. Annual allowances vary internationally and are typically in the range 2% to 5% of the capital cost per annum, which are applied to cover O&M costs for the system as a whole. GMS percentage allowed will need to be agreed by the RPCC, or by the RPTCC initially. The "operations" element of this component could be increased to cover a contribution to the TSO's overall administration costs.

For dedicated interconnectors such as SPEs or private-owned transmission assets, operating costs could be the actual operating costs as approved by the RPCC/RPTCC.

Step 3: Calculate the use of transmission system and associated transmission losses for each regional bilateral trade

Step 3 determines the extent of use of each of the transmission assets and the associated transmission losses for each regional bilateral trade. A load flow-based approach is proposed for this calculation.

When a new regional wheeling trade is proposed, the RPCC or RPTCC will need to commission a load flow, contingency analysis, and dynamic stability study to ensure that there is sufficient transmission access for the regional bilateral trade before it is approved.

A base case load flow is then required to assess the impact of the trade on the system for charging purposes. Wheeling charges should be based on the contribution that wheeling power flows make to the maximum loading of the transmission network. It is the peak loading on the transmission assets that determines the transmission capacity required on the network and hence drives transmission investment costs. Generally, the power system experiences peak transmission loads at the time of maximum demand, and so for each year, a load flow should be undertaken for the forecast maximum generation hour.

The transmission pricing and losses studies should be performed annually by RPCC planning engineers. The basic steps are:

(i) Set up base case simulation model with the peak demands and generation in the region including all the proposed regional bilateral trades.
(ii) Remove a regional bilateral trade by decreasing the consumption by the trade volume at the transmission node associated with the demand (or at the border between countries). The order for the regional bilateral trades is, the oldest trade is applied to the methodology first to be aligned with open access rules. The associated generator is set to be the swing bus. Solve the DC load flow with the bilateral trade removed. (Note that a DC load flow methodology is proposed, as the AC load flow will give incorrect results due to voltage changes and subsequent changes in voltage dependent loads).
(iii) Add the regional bilateral trade back by increasing the consumption by the trade volume at the transmission node associated with the demand. The associated generator is set to be the swing bus. Solve the DC load flow.
(iv) As the trade is added, the transmission elements at voltage levels ≥ 110 kV that increase their flow by more than 1% are recorded and classed as the transmission assets utilized for the specific regional bilateral trade.
(v) The change in transmission losses is calculated by subtracting the trade volume from the generation increase. If the result is positive, then this is the expected transmission losses.

If the value is negative, then the bilateral trade reduces transmission losses and a policy decision is required as to whether the losses charge is set to zero or becomes a credit in this case.

Tx losses = Δ Generation - Regional Bilateral Trade Volume

where Tx losses means transmission losses and Δ Generation means the change in generation.

The calculation of losses could be performed for different periods of the day and year to obtain average losses. This would require accurate models for each period, and will depend on the degree of variation of the flow patterns on the network that is providing the wheeling service.

(vi) Repeat steps b to e for each regional bilateral trade in order, beginning with the earliest established trade.

It would be possible to develop indicative costs for future regional bilateral trades by using the load flow model and simulating generation and off-take points throughout the network. Most load flow simulation packages allow for macros to be written for multiple studies such as this.

Step 4: Calculate transmission revenue requirements for each TSO for regional bilateral trades

The calculation of the revenue requirements for each TSO that is providing wheeling services is undertaken to ensure they receive the revenue requirement corresponding to the use of the assets that has been made. The costs can be attributed to each wheeling transaction, based on its contribution to the use of each of the assets on the TSO's network, where the revenue requirement for each asset is derived from the procedure described in Step 2.

The apportioning is calculated on the percentage use of each asset for regional trades of the transmission network to the total energy flow multiplied by the revenue requirements for the regional asset. This percentage use is calculated by expressing the wheeling flow on each asset as a proportion of its maximum loading.

$$\text{TSO bilateral asset revenue (i)} = \sum_{j=1}^{m} (\text{TSO regional bilateral trade percentage for asset (i, j)/100)} * \text{TSO revenue requirement for asset (i))}$$

where,

j = a regional bilateral trade;

m = the total number of regional bilateral trades; and

i = every transmission asset used for regional bilateral trades in TSO.

The TSO revenue requirements for assets (i) is determined in step 2. The TSO regional bilateral trade portion for each trade (j) and each asset (i) is determined in step 3.

This allocates the portion of the network utilized by all of the regional bilateral trades for each transmission asset in each TSO.

The sum of all the bilateral assets' portions in TSO is the total revenue due to the TSO:

$$\text{TSO annual revenue (k)} = \sum_{i=1}^{n} \text{TSO bilateral asset revenue (i)}$$

where,

n = the total regional interconnection assets in the TSO (k).

The calculation is repeated for each TSO in the interconnection.

Dedicated wheeling assets
For a transmission line that is specifically built for a single regional trade, the TSO regional bilateral trade percentage will by definition be 100% for each transmission asset on the line.

This will ensure that the revenue requirement is fully met, (i.e., the asset cost is fully recovered from the wheeling trade), the full TSO costs are covered, and revenue is guaranteed.

Losses
Transmission losses are paid as "TSO loss factor multiplied by the regional bilateral trade times the price for the energy lost." The RPCC will determine the applicable energy price to be used in loss valuation.

$$\text{TSO transmission losses revenue (k)} = \sum_{j=1}^{m} \text{transmission flow for bilateral trade (j)} * \alpha \text{ (j)} * \text{energy price}$$

Where

α (j) is the loss factor for bilateral trade j

Step 5: Calculate transmission tariff and transmission losses for the purchaser of each regional bilateral trade

Transmission tariff
The sum of the individual asset costs for each bilateral transaction will be paid by the purchaser of the regional bilateral trade. (This is proposed as the convention for ease of settlement; however, it would be possible for the wheeling charge to be split between the load and the generation associated with the specific bilateral trade.)

Therefore, the wheeling charge for a given transaction (j) is calculated as:

$$\text{TSO bilateral asset revenue (j)} = \sum_{j=1}^{n} (\text{TSO regional bilateral trade percentage for asset (i, j)/100)} * \text{TSO revenue requirement for asset (i))}$$

The required revenue to the TSO from the transaction can be converted into a rate charged per kWh based on the hourly scheduled (contracted) energy associated with the bilateral contract.

Losses payment
The costs of transmission losses are paid by the purchaser of the regional bilateral trade. The price payable for the energy should be determined by the RPCC. Alternatively, the generation schedule for the seller of the regional bilateral trade can be increased by the transmission losses percentage, if an "in kind" arrangement for settling losses is adopted.

RPCC/RPTCC role in revenue collection, payments, and RPCC funding

The RPCC will collect from purchasers of bilateral trades both the wheeling tariff and the transmission losses element. A percentage mark-up should be applied to pay for banking charges.

The RPCC will then be responsible for paying to the TSOs their allocated wheeling charges and losses revenue.

Billing and settlements are based on energy schedules (or actual flows), which will be provided by the purchaser of the regional bilateral trade and reconciled by the RPCC.

Billing and settlements should be undertaken monthly, or at such other frequency decided by the RPCC.

Taking responsibility for funds transfer would not be possible for the RPTCC under its current constitution, thus this will require the creation of a new entity to act as the settlement agent for energy trades and wheeling charges in the future.

Other issues

- **Congestion management.** Congestion is managed on a first-come-first-served basis. The latest signed regional bilateral trade will be the first to be curtailed.
- **Ancillary services costs.** Any specialized transmission device deemed as ancillary service will be settled by the trading parties directly.

Appendix 5: Application of Wheeling Charge Methodology - Use of Existing Network Assets

This section provides a simplified theoretical example of a 100 MW bilateral trade from Myanmar to Cambodia via Thailand. The trade is a fixed 100 MW through the year. The network for this example is assumed to have the simplified configuration as shown in Figure A5.1.

The steps in the methodology are followed only for the lines involved in the transaction to show how the methodology works.

Figure A5.1: Simplified Network for 100 MW Transaction between Myanmar and Cambodia

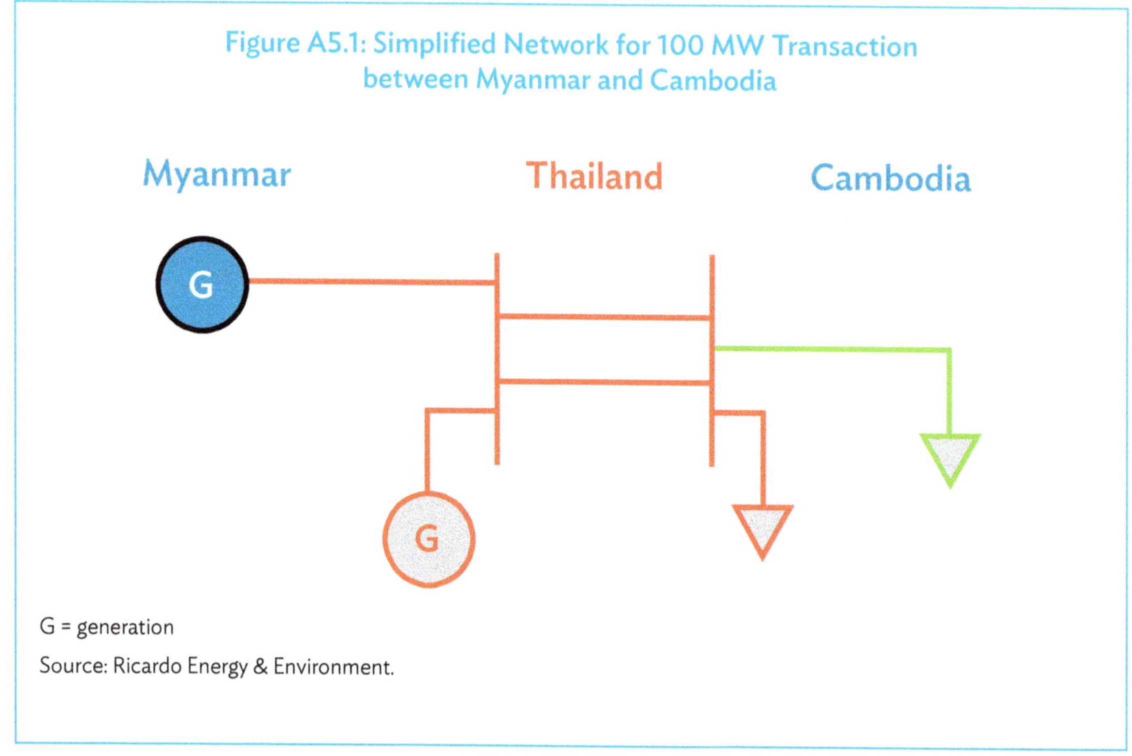

G = generation

Source: Ricardo Energy & Environment.

Step 1: Determine the regional transmission assets and asset value

The Regional Transmission Network for this example is the four transmission lines shown in Section E-1:

- One transmission line connecting Myanmar to Thailand with an assumed replacement value of $10 million;
- Two transmission lines internally in Thailand network with replacement values of $100 million each; and
- One transmission line connecting Thailand to Cambodia with a replacement value of $10 million (Figure A5.2).

Figure A5.2: Simplified Network Showing the Transmission Asset Values

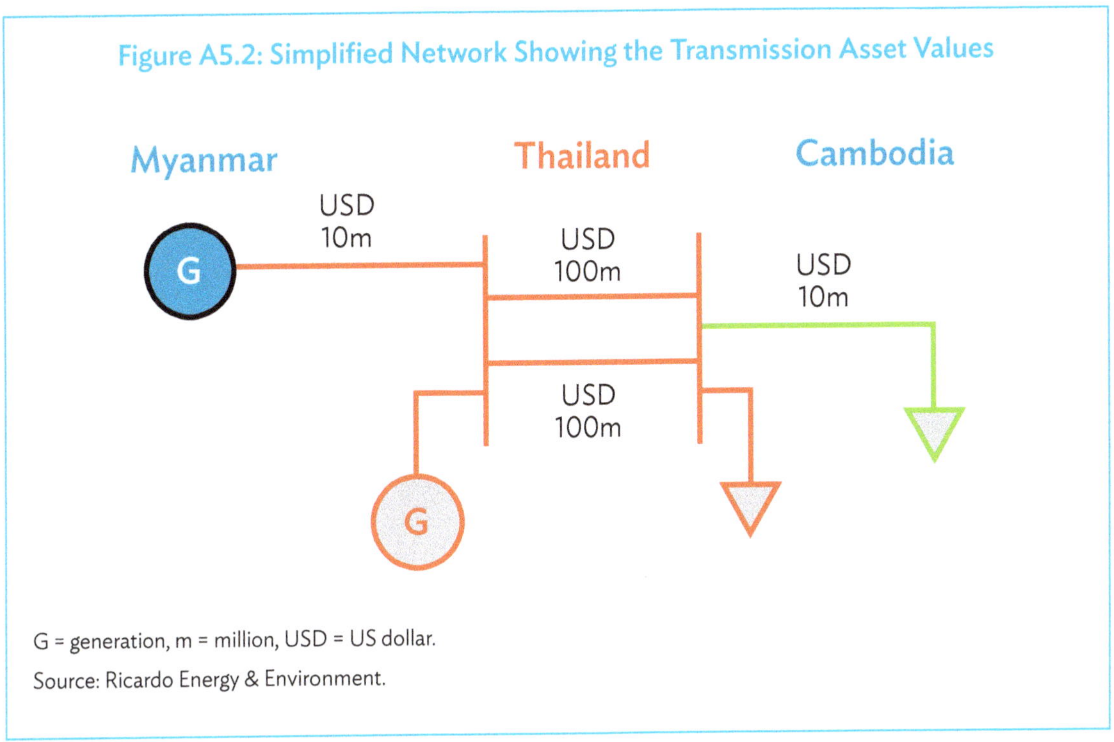

G = generation, m = million, USD = US dollar.

Source: Ricardo Energy & Environment.

Step 2: Calculate annual revenue requirements for each transmission system operator asset used for regional bilateral trading

The cost components to be recovered are capital costs of network plant and equipment, and operation and maintenance costs.

The method for calculating annual asset value is the depreciated replacement cost.

In this simple example, the annual revenue required to be recovered for capital, maintenance, and operating costs is assumed to be 10% of the asset value, as shown in Figure A5.3.

Figure A5.3: Simplified Network Showing the Transmission Asset Annual Revenue Requirements

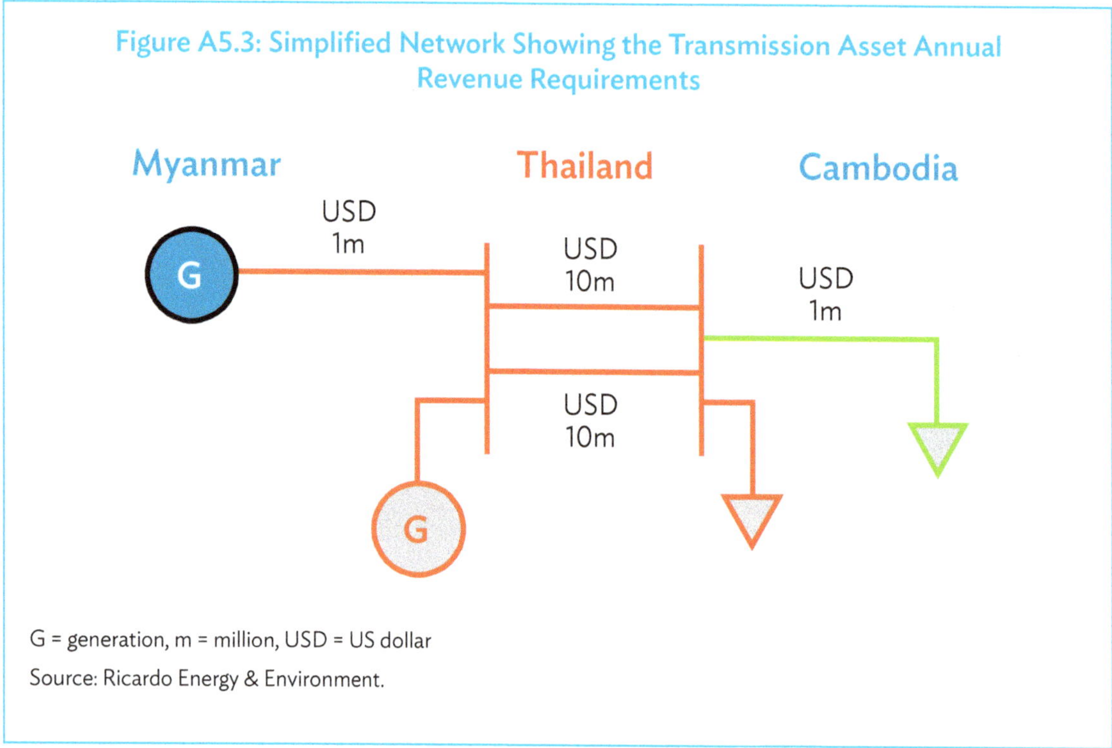

G = generation, m = million, USD = US dollar

Source: Ricardo Energy & Environment.

Step 3: Calculate use of transmission system and associated transmission losses for each regional bilateral trade

Step 3 determines the transmission assets utilized and the associated transmission losses for each regional bilateral trade.

The basic steps are:

(i) Set up base case simulation model with the peak demands and generation in the region, including all of the regional bilateral trades.

(ii) Remove a regional bilateral trade by decreasing the consumption by the trade volume at the transmission node associated with the demand (or at the border between countries). The associated generator is set to be the swing bus. Solve the direct current (DC) load flow. In the simplified example in Figure A5.4, a generator provides 1000 MW of demand within Thailand. Note that there is 30 MW of losses in this example.

(iii) Add the regional bilateral trade back by increasing the consumption by the trade volume at the transmission node associated with the demand. The associated generator is set to be the swing bus. Solve the DC load flow (Figure A5.5).

(iv) As the trade is added, the transmission elements that changed by more than 1% are noted as the transmission assets utilized for the specific regional bilateral trade. All the assets are utilized in this simplified example, and the percentage usage is shown in Table A5.1.

Figure A5.4: Load Flow Solution without Bilateral Transaction

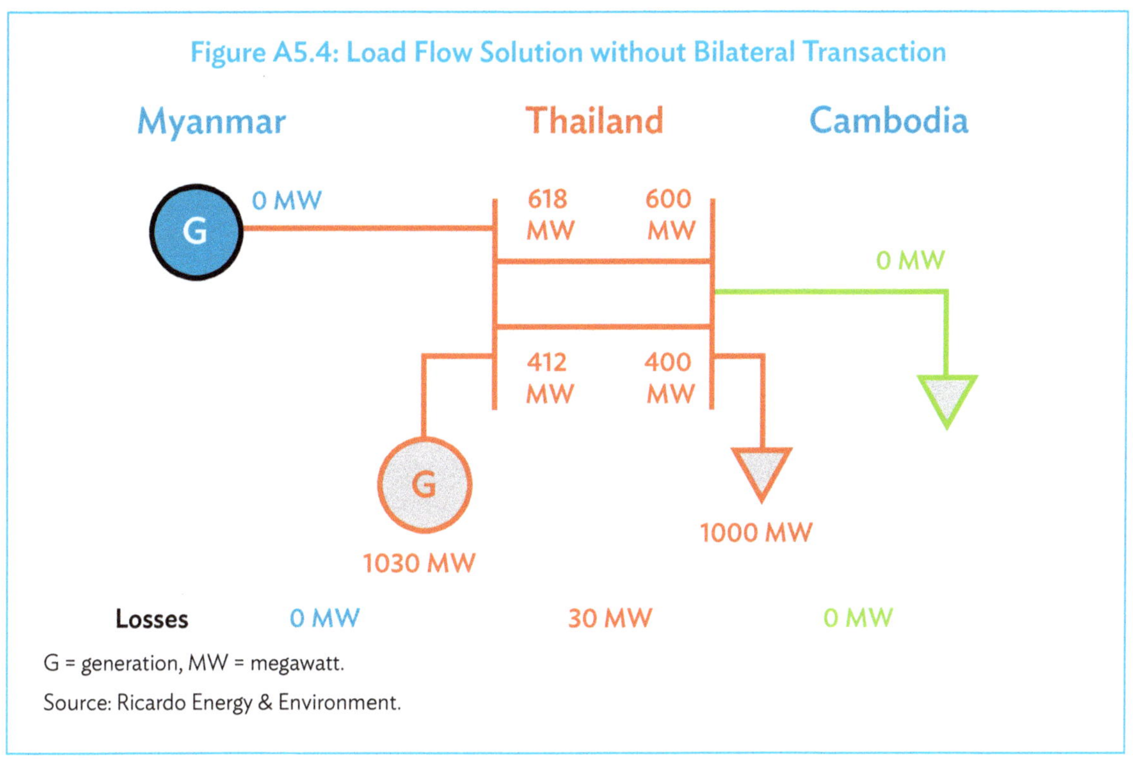

G = generation, MW = megawatt.

Source: Ricardo Energy & Environment.

Figure A5.5: Load Flow Solution with Bilateral Transaction

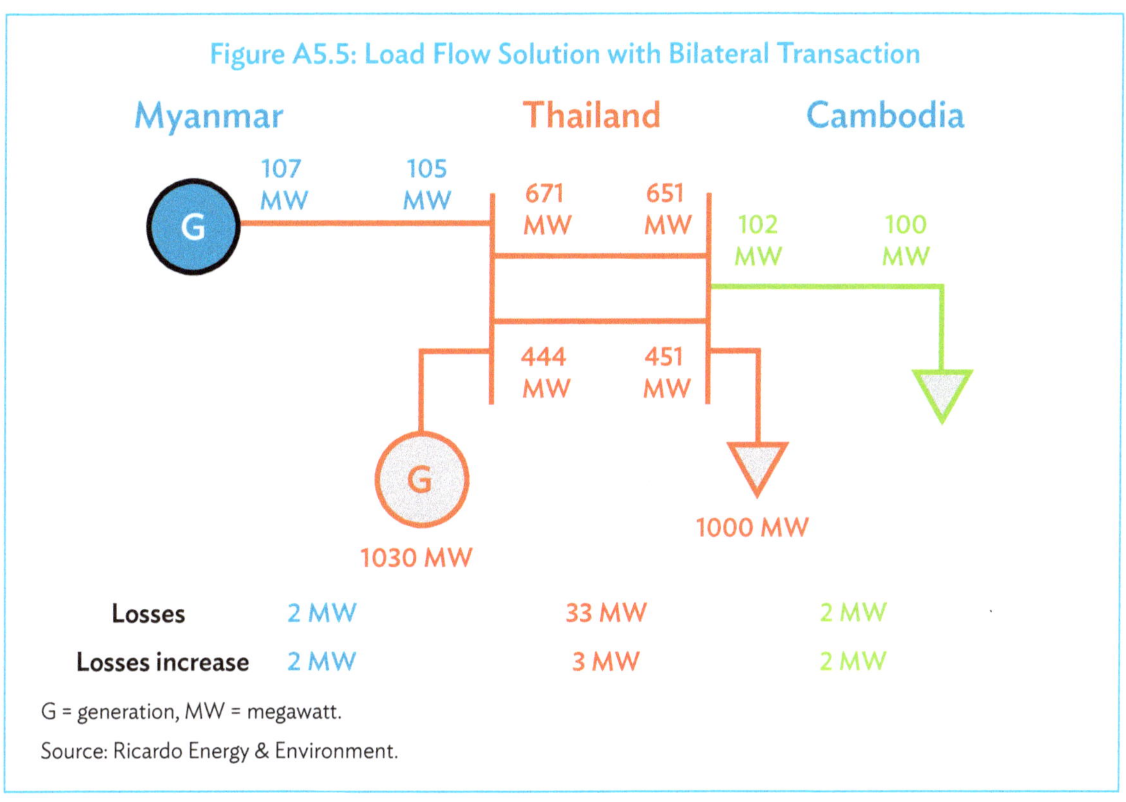

G = generation, MW = megawatt.

Source: Ricardo Energy & Environment.

Table A5.1: Changes in line flows after addition of 100 MW load

	Myanmar	Thailand		Cambodia
Line number	L1	L1	L2	L1
Change in flow on line (MW)	107	53	52	102
Total flow (MW)	107	671	444	102
Usage	100%	7.9%	11.7%	100%

L = line, MW = megawatt.

Source: Ricardo Energy & Environment.

(v) The change in transmission losses is calculated by subtracting the trade volume from the generation increase. If the result is positive, then this is the expected transmission losses.

Tx losses = Δ Generation – Regional Bilateral Trade

= 107 MW – 100 MW = 7 MW.

where Tx losses means transmission losses and Δ Generation means the change in generation.

(vi) Repeat steps b to e for each regional bilateral trade in order, from the oldest trade first.

Step 4: Calculate transmission revenue requirements for each TSO for regional bilateral trades

The calculation of the revenue requirements for each TSO will ensure that they receive their full revenue requirement, and the costs are then apportioned to each user of the system.

The apportioning is calculated on the percentage use of each asset for regional trades of the transmission network to the total energy flow multiplied by the revenue requirements for the regional asset.

$$\text{TSO bilateral asset revenue (i)} = \sum_{j=1}^{m} \text{(TSO regional bilateral trade percentage for asset (i, j)/100)} * \text{TSO revenue requirement for asset (i))}$$

Where,

j = a regional bilateral trade,

m = the total number of regional bilateral trades, and

i = every transmission asset used for regional bilateral trades in TSO.

Table A5.2 shows the revenue calculations for each country.

Table A5.2: Calculation of Transmission Revenue Requirements

	Myanmar	Thailand		Cambodia
Line number	L1	L1	L2	L1
Annual revenue requirement per line ($ million)	1	10	10	1
Bilateral trade usage	100%	7.9%	11.7%	100%
Revenue from bilateral trade ($ million)	1	0.79	1.17	1
Total revenue to TSO ($ million)	1	1.96		1

L = line

Source: Ricardo Energy & Environment.

Transmission losses are paid as the TSO loss factor multiplied by the regional bilateral trade times the price for the energy lost.

$$\text{TSO transmission losses revenue (k)} = \sum_{j=1}^{m} \text{transmission flow for bilateral trade (j)} * \alpha \text{ (j)} * \text{energy price}$$

Where

α (j) = the loss factor for bilateral trade j.

In the sample case, the loss factors for the 100 MW bilateral trade are as follows:

	Myanmar	Thailand	Cambodia
Change in losses on line (MW)	2	3	2
Loss factor	2%	3%	2%

Step 5: Calculate the transmission tariff and transmission losses for the purchaser of each regional bilateral trade

The sum of the individual asset costs for each bilateral charge is paid by the purchaser of the regional bilateral trade:

$$\text{TSO bilateral asset revenue (j)} = \sum_{i=1}^{n} (\text{TSO regional bilateral trade percentage for asset (i, j)/100)} * \text{TSO revenue requirement for asset (i))}$$

The bilateral trade in this case has to pay a total of $3.96 million.

The example assumes that the 100 MW will be provided the whole year, thus the energy provided over the year = 100 MW * 365 days * 24 hrs = 876,000 MWh.

The transmission price for the energy is thus calculated as:

Purchaser Tx charge = $3,960,000 / 876,000 MWh = $4.5 / MWh

where Tx charge means transmission charge.

The costs are charged at rate per kWh based on hourly scheduled (contracted) energy.

The transmission losses are paid by the purchaser of the regional bilateral trade. The price payable for the energy is determined by the RPCC. Alternatively, the seller of the regional bilateral trade's generation schedule is increased by the transmission losses percentage.

www.ingramcontent.com/pod-product-compliance
Lightning Source LLC
Chambersburg PA
CBHW041120280326
41928CB00061B/3471
9789292620363